Praise for Er  t

"What we learn from Eros the Bittersweet while being spun alive by its brilliance is that its author is a philosopher of much cunning and an agile reader, a scholar with a mind as fresh as a spring meadow, no dust anywhere on her."—Guy Davenport

"Highly recommended."—Choice

"There is a fine beauty to the work, and it deserves reading."—Library Journal

eros

the bittersweet

anne carson

Dalkey Archive Press

normal · london

First Dalkey Archive edition, 1998
Second printing, 2000
Third printing, 2003
Fourth printing, 2005
All rights reserved

Library of Congress Cataloging-in-Publication Data:

Carson, Anne, 1950-
    Eros the bittersweet / by Anne Carson. — 1st Dalkey Archive ed.
            p.   cm.
    Originally published: Princeton, N.J. : Princeton University Press, c1986.
    Includes bibliographical references and index.
    ISBN 1-56478-188-7 (alk. paper)
    1. Eros (Greek deity)   2. Love.   I. Title.
    BL820.C65C37   1998   880.9'3543—dc21   97-51954

This publication is partially supported by grants from the Lannan Foundation,
the National Endowment for the Arts, a federal agency, and the Illinois Arts
Council, a state agency.

Dalkey Archive Press is a nonprofit organization located at Milner Library (Illinois State
University) and distributed in the UK by Turnaround Publisher Services Ltd. (London).

www.dalkeyarchive.com

Printed on permanent/durable acid-free paper and bound in the United States
of America.

Contents

Contents

Abbreviations

Aesch.	Aeschylus
Ag.	*Agamemnon*
PV	*Prometheus Bound*
Sept.	*Seven against Thebes*
Supp.	*Suppliants*
Anac.	*Elegy and Iambus . . . with the Anacreontea*, ed. J. M. Edmonds (Cambridge, Mass., 1961)
Anth. Pal.	*The Greek Anthology*, ed. W. R. Paton, 5 vols. (London and New York, 1916)
Ap. Rhod.	Apollonius Rhodius, *Argonautica*, ed. R. C. Seaton (Oxford, 1900)
Ar.	Aristophanes
Eccl.	*Ecclesiazusae*
Nub.	*Clouds*
Ran.	*Frogs*
Arist.	Aristotle
De An.	*On the Soul*
Metaph. A	*Metaphysics A*
Ph.	*Physics*
Poet.	*Poetics*
Pol.	*Politics*
Rh.	*Rhetoric*
Sens.	*On the Senses*

Ath.	Athenaios, *Deipnosophistae*, ed. G. Kaibel, 3 vols. (Leipzig, 1887-1890)
CAF	*Comicorum Atticorum Fragmenta*, ed. T. Kock, 3 vols. (Leipzig, 1880-1888)
Diels, *VS.*	*Die Fragmente der Vorsokratiker*, ed. H. Diels, 3 vols. (Berlin, 1959-1960)
Eur.	Euripides
Hipp.	*Hippolytus*
IA	*Iphigeneia at Aulis*
Sthen.	*Sthenoboea*
FGrH	*Fragmenta Graecorum Historicorum*, ed. F. Jacoby, 15 vols. (Berlin and Leiden, 1923-1958)
Hilgard, *Gramm. Gr.*	*Grammatici Graeci*, ed. A. Hilgard, 3 vols. (Leipzig, 1901)
Hom.	Homer
Il.	*Iliad*
Od.	*Odyssey*
LP	*Poetarum Lesbiorum Fragmenta*, ed. E. Lobel and D. Page (Oxford, 1955)
LSJ	Liddell and Scott, *Greek-English Lexicon*, 9th ed., rev. Jones (Oxford, 1968)
Pind.	Pindar
Pyth.	*Pythian Odes*
Pl.	Plato
Ap.	*Apology*
Phdr.	*Phaedrus*
Phlb.	*Philebus*
Soph.	*Sophist*
Symp.	*Symposium*

Theag.	*Theages*
Tht.	*Theaetetus*
PMG	*Poetae Melici Graeci*, ed. D. Page (Oxford, 1962)
Radt	*Tragicorum Graecorum Fragmenta IV: Sophocles*, ed. S. Radt (Göttingen, 1977)
Snell-Maehler	*Pindari Carmina cum Fragmentis*, ed. B. Snell and H. Maehler, 2 vols. (Leipzig, 1971)
Soph.	Sophokles
Ant.	*Antigone*
OC	*Oedipus at Colonus*
Trach.	*Trachiniae*
Stob., *Flor.*	*Ioannis Stobaei Florilegium*, ed. T. Gaisford, 4 vols. (Oxford, 1822)
TGF	*Tragicorum Graecorum Fragmenta*, ed. A. Nauck, 2nd ed. (Leipzig, 1889)
West, *IEG*	*Iambi et Elegi Graeci*, ed. M. L. West, 2 vols. (Oxford, 1971-1972)

Preface

Kafka's "The Top" is a story about a philosopher who spends his spare time around children so he can grab their tops in spin. To catch a top still spinning makes him happy for a moment in his belief "that the understanding of any detail, that of a spinning top for instance, was sufficient for the understanding of all things." Disgust follows delight almost at once and he throws down the top, walks away. Yet hope of understanding continues to fill him each time top-spinning preparations begin among the children: "as soon as the top began to spin and he was running breathlessly after it, the hope would turn to certainty but when he held the silly piece of wood in his hand he felt nauseated."

The story is about the delight we take in metaphor. A meaning spins, remaining upright on an axis of normalcy aligned with the conventions of connotation and denotation, and yet: to spin is not normal, and to dissemble normal uprightness by means of this fantastic motion is impertinent. What is the relation of impertinence to the hope of understanding? To delight?

The story concerns the reason why we love to fall in love. Beauty spins and the mind moves. To catch beauty would be to understand how that impertinent stability in vertigo is possible. But no, delight need not reach so far. To be running breathlessly, but not yet arrived, is itself delightful, a suspended moment of living hope.

Suppression of impertinence is not the lover's aim. Nor can I believe this philosopher really runs after understanding. Rather, he has become a philosopher (that is, one whose profession is to delight in understanding) in order to furnish himself with pretexts for running after tops.

Princeton, New Jersey
August 1985

eros
the bittersweet

Bittersweet

It was Sappho who first called eros "bittersweet." No one who has been in love disputes her. What does the word mean? Eros seemed to Sappho at once an experience of pleasure and pain. Here is contradiction and perhaps paradox. To perceive this eros can split the mind in two. Why? The components of the contradiction may seem, at first glance, obvious. We take for granted, as did Sappho, the sweetness of erotic desire; its pleasurability smiles out at us. But the bitterness is less obvious. There might be several reasons why what is sweet should also be bitter. There may be various relations between the two savors. Poets have sorted the matter out in different ways. Sappho's own formulation is a good place to begin tracing the possibilities. The relevant fragment runs:

Ἔρος δηὖτέ μ' ὁ λυσιμέλης δόνει,
γλυκύπικρον ἀμάχανον ὄρπετον

Eros once again limb-loosener whirls me
sweetbitter, impossible to fight off, creature stealing up
(LP, fr. 130)

It is hard to translate. "Sweetbitter" sounds wrong, and yet our standard English rendering "bittersweet" inverts the actual terms of Sappho's compound *glukupikron*. Should that concern us? If her ordering has a descriptive intention, eros is here being said to bring sweetness, then bitterness in sequence: she is sorting the possibilities chronologically. Many a lover's experience would validate such a chronology, especially in poetry, where most love ends badly. But it is unlikely that this is what Sappho means. Her poem begins with a dramatic localization of the erotic situation in time (*dēute*) and fixes the erotic action in the present indicative tense (*donei*). She is not recording the history of a love affair but the instant of desire. One moment staggers under pressure of eros; one mental state splits. A simultaneity of pleasure and pain is at issue. The pleasant aspect is named first, we may presume, because it is less surprising. Emphasis is thrown upon the problematic other side of the phenomenon, whose attributes advance in a hail of soft consonants (line 2). Eros moves or creeps upon its victim from somewhere outside her: *orpeton*. No battle avails to fight off that advance: *amachanon*. Desire, then, is neither inhabitant nor ally of the desirer. Foreign to her will, it forces itself irresistibly upon her from without. Eros is an enemy. Its bitterness must be the taste of enmity. That would be hate.

"To love one's friends and hate one's enemies" is a standard archaic prescription for moral response. Love and hate construct between them the machinery of human contact. Does it make sense to locate both poles of this affect within the single emotional event of eros? Presumably, yes, if friend and enemy converge in the being who is its occasion. The convergence creates a paradox, but one that is almost a cliché for the modern literary imagination. "And hate begins where love leaves off . . ." whispers Anna Karenina, as she heads for Moscow Station and an end to the dilemma of desire. In fact, erotic paradox is a problem antedating Eros himself. We find it first enacted on the wall of Troy, in a scene between Helen and Aphrodite. The interchange is as sharp as a paradigm. Homer shows us Helen, embodiment of desire, fed up with the impositions of eros and defying an order from Aphrodite to serve Paris' bed. The goddess of

love responds angrily, wielding erotic paradox as a
weapon:

μή μ᾽ ἔρεθε σχετλίη, μὴ χωσαμένη σε μεθείω,
τὼς δέ σ᾽ ἀπεχθήρω ὡς νῦν ἔκπαγλ᾽ ἐφίλησα

Damn you woman, don't provoke me—I'll get angry
and let you drop!
I'll come to hate you as terribly as I now love you!
(*Il.* 3.414-15)

Helen obeys at once; love and hate in combination make
an irresistible enemy.

The simultaneity of bitter and sweet that startles us in
Sappho's adjective *glukupikron* is differently rendered in
Homer's poem. Epic convention represents inner states
of feeling in dynamic and linear enactment, so that a divided mind may be read from a sequence of antithetical
actions. Homer and Sappho concur, however, in present-
ing the divinity of desire as an ambivalent being, at once
friend and enemy, who informs the erotic experience
with emotional paradox.

Eros appears in other genres and poets, too, as a paradox of love and hate. Aristophanes, for example, tells us
that the seductive young libertine Alkibiades was able to
inspire a feeling like lover's passion in the Greek *dēmos*:

ποθεῖ μέν, ἐχθαίρει δέ, βούλεται δ᾽ ἔχειν.

For they love him and they hate him
and they long to possess him.
(*Ran.* 1425)

In Aeschylus' *Agamemnon*, Menelaos is described wan-
dering about his empty palace after the departure of
Helen. The rooms seem haunted by her; at their bed-
chamber he stops and cries out for "ruts of love in the
bed" (411). There is no question it is desire he feels (*pothos*, 414), yet hate seeps in to fill the void (*echthetai*):

· 5 ·

πόθῳ δ᾽ ὑπερποντίας
φάσμα δόξει δόμων ἀνάσσειν·
εὐμόρφων δὲ κολοσσῶν
ἔχθεται χάρις ἀνδρί,
ὀμμάτων δ᾽ ἐν ἀχηνίαις
ἔρρει πᾶς ᾽Αφροδίτα.

Because of his longing for something gone across
   the sea
a phantom seems to rule the rooms,
and the grace of statues shaped in beauty
comes to be an object of hate for the man.
In the absences of eyes
   all Aphrodite is vacant, gone.
                              (*Ag.* 414-19)

Love and hate furnish a subject for the Hellenistic epigram as well. Nicharchos' injunction to his beloved is typical:

Εἴ με φιλεῖς, μισεῖς με· καὶ εἰ μισεῖς, σὺ φιλεῖς με·
   εἰ δέ με μὴ μισεῖς, φίλτατε, μή με φίλει.

If you love me, you hate me. And if you hate me, you
   love me.
Now if you don't hate me, beloved, don't love me.
                              (*Anth. Pal.* 11.252)

Catullus' epigram is perhaps the most elegant distillate we have of this cliché:

Odi et amo. quare id faciam, fortasse requiris.
   nescio, sed fieri sentio et excrucior.

I hate and I love. Why? you might ask.
   I don't know. But I feel it happening and I hurt.
                              (Catullus 85)

The poets of the Greek lyric tradition sometimes conceptualize the erotic condition as starkly as this, but Sappho and her successors in general prefer physiology to concepts. The moment when the soul parts on itself in desire is conceived as a dilemma of body and senses. On Sappho's tongue, as we have seen, it is a moment bitter and sweet. This ambivalent taste is developed, in later poets, into "bitter honey" (*Anth. Pal.* 12.81), "sweet wound" (*Anth. Pal.* 12.126), and "Eros of sweet tears" (*Anth. Pal.* 12.167). Eros knocks a lover flat with the shock of hot and cold in Anakreon's poem:

μεγάλῳ δηὖτέ μ᾽ Ἔρως ἔκοψεν ὥστε χαλκεὺς
πελέκει, χειμερίῃ δ᾽ ἔλουσεν χαράδρῃ.

With his huge hammer again Eros knocked me like a
    blacksmith
and doused me in a wintry ditch
(*PMG* 413)

while Sophokles compares the experience to a lump of ice melting in warm hands (Radt, fr. 149).[1] Later poets mix the sensations of hot and cold with the metaphor from taste to concoct "sweet fire" (*Anth. Pal.* 12.63), lovers "burned by honey" (*Anth. Pal.* 12.126), erotic missiles "tempered in honey" (Anac. 27E). Ibykos frames eros in a paradox of wet and dry, for the black thunderstorm of desire drives against him not rain but "parching madnesses" (*PMG* 286.8-11). These tropes may have some basis in ancient theories of physiology and psychology, which associate action that is pleasurable, desirable or good with sensations of heat, liquidity, melting, and action that is unpleasant or hateful with cold, freezing, rigidification.

But no simple map of the emotions is available here. Desire is not simple. In Greek the act of love is a mingling (*mignumi*) and desire melts the limbs (*lusimelēs*, cf. Sappho fr. 130 above). Boundaries of body, categories of thought, are confounded. The god who melts limbs pro-

[1] See also the section on "Ice-pleasure" in the Sophoklean fragment below.

ceeds to break the lover (*damnatai*) as would a foe on the epic battlefield:

ἀλλά μ᾽ ὁ λυσιμελὴς ὦταῖρε δάμναται πόθος.

Oh comrade, the limb-loosener crushes me: desire.

(Archilochos, West, *IEG* 196)

The shape of love and hate is perceptible, then, in a variety of sensational crises. Each crisis calls for decision and action, but decision is impossible and action a paradox when eros stirs the senses. Everyday life can become difficult; the poets speak of the consequences for behavior and judgment:

οὐκ οἶδ ὄττι θέω· δίχα μοι τὰ νοήμματα

I don't know what I should do: two states of mind
   in me. . . .

(*LP*, fr. 51)

Sappho says, and breaks off.

ἐρέω τε δηὖτε κοὐκ ἐρέω
καὶ μαίνομαι κοὐ μαίνομαι.

I'm in love! I'm not in love!
I'm crazy! I'm not crazy!
      (*PMG* 428)

cries Anakreon.

ἐξ οὗ δὴ νέον ἔρνος ἐν ἠϊθέοις Διόφαντον
λεύσσων οὔτε φυγεῖν οὔτε μένειν δύναμαι.

When I look at Diophantos, new shoot among the
   young men,
   I can neither flee nor stay
   (*Anth. Pal.* 12.126.5-6)

"Desire keeps pulling the lover to act and not to act" is the conclusion of Sophokles (Radt, fr. 149). Not only action founders. Moral evaluation also fractures under pressure of paradox, splitting desire into a thing good and bad at the same time. The Eros of Euripides wields a bow that is "double" in its effect, for it can bring on a lovely life or complete collapse (*IA* 548-49). Euripides goes so far as to double the god of love himself: twin Erotes appear in a fragment of his lost play *Sthenoboea*. One of them guides the lover in a life of virtue. The other is a lover's worst enemy (*echthistos*) and leads him straight to the house of death (Page 1932, 3.128.22-25). Love and hate bifurcate Eros.

Let us return to the question with which we began, namely, the meaning of Sappho's adjective *glukupikron*. A contour has been emerging from our examination of the poetic texts. "Sweetbitter eros" is what hits the raw film of the lover's mind. Paradox is what takes shape on the sensitized plate of the poem, a negative image from which positive pictures can be created. Whether apprehended as a dilemma of sensation, action or value, eros prints as the same contradictory fact: love and hate converge within erotic desire.

Why?

Gone

Perhaps there are many ways to answer this. One comes clearest in Greek. The Greek word *eros* denotes 'want,' 'lack,' 'desire for that which is missing.' The lover wants what he does not have. It is by definition impossible for him to have what he wants if, as soon as it is had, it is no longer wanting. This is more than wordplay. There is a dilemma within eros that has been thought crucial by thinkers from Sappho to the present day. Plato turns and returns to it. Four of his dialogues explore what it means to say that desire can only be for what is lacking, not at hand, not present, not in one's possession nor in one's being: *eros* entails *endeia*. As Diotima puts it in the *Symposium*, Eros is a bastard got by Wealth on Poverty and ever at home in a life of want (203b-e). Hunger is the analog chosen by Simone Weil for this conundrum:

> All our desires are contradictory, like the desire for food. I want the person I love to love me. If he is, however, totally devoted to me he does not exist any longer and I cease to love him. And as long as he is not totally devoted to me he does not love me enough. Hunger and repletion. (1977, 364)

Emily Dickinson puts the case more pertly in "I Had Been Hungry":

> So I found
> that hunger was a way
> of persons outside windows
> that entering takes away.

Gone

Petrarch interprets the problem in terms of the ancient physiology of fire and ice:

I know to follow while I flee my fire
I freeze when present; when absent, hot is my desire.
("Trionfo d'Amore")

Sartre has less patience with the contradictory ideal of desire, this "dupery." He sees in erotic relations a system of infinite reflections, a deceiving mirror-game that carries within itself its own frustration (1956, 444-45). For Simone de Beauvoir the game is torture: "The knight departing for new adventures offends his lady yet she has nothing but contempt for him if he remains at her feet. This is the torture of impossible love . . ." (1953, 619). Jacques Lacan puts the matter somewhat more enigmatically when he says "Desire . . . evokes lack of being under the three figures of the nothing that constitutes the basis of the demand for love, of the hate that even denies the other's being, and of the unspeakable element in that which is ignored in its request" (1966, 28).

It would seem that these various voices are pursuing a common perception. All human desire is poised on an axis of paradox, absence and presence its poles, love and hate its motive energies. Let us return once more to the poem of Sappho with which we began. This fragment (*LP*, fr. 130), as it is preserved in the text and scholia of Hephaestion, is followed without a break by two lines in the same meter, which may be from the same poem:

Ἄτθι, σοὶ δ' ἔμεθεν μὲν ἀπήχθετο
φροντίσδην, ἐπὶ δ' Ἀνδρομέδαν πόται

Atthis, your care for me stirred hatred in you
and you flew to Andromeda.
(*LP*, fr. 131)

Who ever desires what is not gone? No one. The Greeks were clear on this. They invented eros to express it.

· 11 ·

Ruse

Let no one enter here who is ignorant of geometry.

(inscription over the door of Plato's Academy)

There is something pure and indubitable about the notion that eros is lack. Moreover, it is a notion that, once adopted, has a powerful effect on one's habits and representations of love. We can see this most clearly in an example: consider Sappho's fragment 31, which is one of the best-known love poems in our tradition.

φαίνεταί μοι κῆνος ἴσος θέοισιν
ἔμμεν' ὤνηρ, ὄττις ἐνάντιός τοι
ἰσδάνει καὶ πλάσιον ἆδυ φωνεί-
σας ὑπακούει

καὶ γελαίσας ἰμέροεν, τό μ' ἦ μὰν
καρδίαν ἐν στήθεσιν ἐπτόαισεν,
ὡς γὰρ ἔς σ' ἴδω βρόχε' ὥς με φώναι-
σ' οὐδ' ἒν ἔτ' εἴκει,

ἀλλ' ἄκαν μὲν γλῶσσα †ἔαγε λέπτον
δ' αὔτικα χρῷ πῦρ ὑπαδεδρόμηκεν,
ὀππάτεσσι δ' οὐδ' ἒν ὄρημμ', ἐπιρρόμ-
βεισι δ' ἄκουαι,

†έκαδε μ' ἴδρως ψῦχρος κακχέεται† τρόμος δὲ
παῖσαν ἄγρει, χλωροτέρα δὲ ποίας
ἔμμι, τεθνάκην δ' ὀλίγω 'πιδεύης
φαίνομ' †αι

He seems to me equal to gods that man
who opposite you

sits and listens close
to your sweet speaking

and lovely laughing—oh it
puts the heart in my chest on wings
for when I look at you, a moment, then no speaking
is left in me

no: tongue breaks, and thin
fire is racing under skin
and in eyes no sight and drumming
fills ears

and cold sweat holds me and shaking
grips me all, greener than grass
I am and dead—or almost
I seem to me.
(*LP*, fr. 31)

The poem floats toward us on a stage set. But we have
no program. The actors go in and out of focus anony-
mously. The action has no location. We don't know why
the girl is laughing nor what she feels about this man. He
looms beyond the footlights, somewhat more than mortal in line 1 (*isos theoisin*), and dissolves at line 2 into a
pronoun (*ottis*) so indefinite that scholars cannot agree
on what it means. The poet who is staging the mise-en-
scène steps mysteriously from the wings of a relative
clause at line 5 (*to*) and takes over the action.

It is not a poem about the three of them as individuals,
but about the geometrical figure formed by their perception of one another, and the gaps in that perception. It is
an image of the distances between them. Thin lines of
force coordinate the three of them. Along one line travels
the girl's voice and laughter to a man who listens closely.
A second tangent connects the girl to the poet. Between
the eye of the poet and the listening man crackles a third
current. The figure is a triangle. Why?

An obvious answer is to say that this is a poem about
jealousy. Numbers of critics have done so. Yet, just as

many readers deny that there is any hint of jealousy here.[2] How is such blanket disagreement possible? Are we all operating with the same idea of what jealousy is?

The word 'jealousy' comes from Greek *zēlos* meaning 'zeal' or 'fervent pursuit.' It is a hot and corrosive spiritual motion arising in fear and fed on resentment. The jealous lover fears that his beloved prefers someone else, and resents any relationship between the beloved and another. This is an emotion concerned with placement and displacement. The jealous lover covets a particular place in the beloved's affection and is full of anxiety that another will take it. Here is an image of the shifting pattern that is jealousy, from more modern times. During the first half of the fifteenth century a type of slow pacing dance called the *bassa danza* became popular in Italy. These dances were semidramatic and transparently expressive of psychological relationships. "In the dance called *Jealousy* three men and three women permute partners and each man goes through a stage of standing by himself apart from the others" (Baxandall 1972, 78). Jealousy is a dance in which everyone moves, for it is the *instability* of the emotional situation that preys upon a jealous lover's mind.

No such permutations jeopardize Sappho in fragment 31. Indeed, her case is the reverse. Were she to change places with the man who listens closely, it seems likely she would be entirely destroyed. She does not covet the man's place nor fear usurpation of her own. She directs no resentment at him. She is simply amazed at his intrepidity. This man's role in the poetic structure reflects that of jealousy within Sappho's feelings. Neither is named. It is the beloved's beauty that affects Sappho; the man's presence is somehow necessary to delineation of that emotional event—it remains to be seen how. "Lovers all

[2] The two most recent commentators on this poem assemble scholarship for and against jealousy: Burnett 1983, 232-43; Race 1983, 92-101.

show such symptoms as these," says Longinus, the ancient critic to whom we owe preservation of Sappho's text (*De Sublimitate* 10.2). Jealousy may be implicit in the symptoms of love whenever they occur, but jealousy does not explain the geometry of this poem.

Another popular theory about fragment 31 is the rhetorical theory, which explains the man who listens closely as a poetic necessity (see note 2). That is, he is not to be thought of as a real person but as a poetic hypothesis, designed to show by contrast how deeply Sappho is affected in the presence of her beloved. As such he is a cliché of erotic poetry, for it is a common rhetorical maneuver to praise one's beloved by saying "He must be made of stone who could resist you." Pindar, for example, in a well-known fragment (Snell-Maehler, fr. 123) contrasts his own response to a beautiful boy ("I melt like wax as the heat bites into it") with that of an impassible observer ("whose black heart was forged of adamant or iron in a cold flame"). The rhetorical point may be reinforced by adding a comparison with divine impassivity, as in the Hellenistic epigram that says "If you looked upon my beloved and were not broken by desire, you are totally god or totally stone" (*Anth. Pal.* 12.151).[3] With this contrastive technique, the lover praises his beloved, and incidentally begs sympathy for his own suit, by aligning himself with normal human response: it would be an unnatural heart or supernatural heart that failed to be moved by desire for such an object. Is this what Sappho is doing in fragment 31?

No. In the first place, the register of normality is missing from Sappho's poem. Her record of erotic emotion is singular. We may recognize her symptoms from personal memory but it is impossible to believe she is representing herself as an ordinary lover. Moreover, praise of the beloved does not stand out as the principal purpose of this

[3] See Dover 1978, 178 n. 18; Race 1983, 93-94.

poem. The girl's voice and laughter are a significant provocation but she disappears at line 5 and Sappho's own body and mind are the unmistakable subject of all that follows. Praise and normal erotic responses are things that occur in the real world: this poem does not. Sappho tells us twice, emphatically, the real location of her poem: "He seems to me. . . . I seem to me." This is a disquisition on seeming and it takes place entirely within her own mind.[4]

Jealousy is beside the point; the normal world of erotic responses is beside the point; praise is beside the point. It is a poem about the lover's mind in the act of constructing desire for itself. Sappho's subject is eros as it *appears* to her; she makes no claim beyond that. A single consciousness represents itself; one mental state is exposed to view.

We see clearly what shape desire has there: a three-point circuit is visible within Sappho's mind. The man who listens closely is no sentimental cliché or rhetorical device. He is a cognitive and intentional necessity. Sappho perceives desire by identifying it *as* a three-part structure. We may, in the traditional terminology of erotic theorizing, refer to this structure as a love triangle and we may be tempted, with post-Romantic asperity, to dismiss it as a ruse. But the ruse of the triangle is not a trivial mental maneuver. We see in it the radical constitution of desire. For, where eros is lack, its activation calls for three structural components—lover, beloved and that which comes between them. They are three points of transformation on a circuit of possible relationship, electrified by desire so that they touch not touching. Conjoined they are held apart. The third component plays a paradoxical role for it both connects and separates, marking that two are not one, irradiating the absence whose presence is demanded by eros. When the cir-

[4] On seeming in this poem, see Robbins 1980, 255-61.

cuit-points connect, perception leaps. And something becomes visible, on the triangular path where volts are moving, that would not be visible without the three-part structure. The difference between what is and what could be is visible. The ideal is projected on a screen of the actual, in a kind of stereoscopy. The man sits like a god, the poet almost dies: two poles of response within the same desiring mind. Triangulation makes both present at once by a shift of distance, replacing erotic action with a ruse of heart and language. For in this dance the people do not move. Desire moves. Eros is a verb.

Tactics

The ruse of inserting a rival between lover and beloved is immediately effective, as Sappho's poem shows, but there are more ways than one to triangulate desire. Not all look triangular in action, yet they share a common concern: to represent eros as deferred, defied, obstructed, hungry, organized around a radiant absence—to represent eros as lack.

Mere space has power. *L'amour d'loonh* ('love from a distance') is what the canny troubadours called courtly love. We have seen Menelaos haunted through his empty palace by "absences of eyes in the statues" (Aesch. *Ag.* 411). With this vacancy we might compare Virgil's *Aeneid*, where the space of desire echoes around Dido in the streets of Carthage:

illum absens absentem auditque uidetque

. . . him not there not there she hears him, she sees him.

(4.83)

A lover like Theognis, on the other hand, neatly accommodates the pain of absent presence, announcing to his boy:

Οὔτε σε κωμάζειν ἀπερύκομεν οὔτε καλοῦμεν·
ἀργαλέος παρεών, καὶ φίλος εὖτ᾽ ἂν ἀπῇς.

We aren't shutting you out of the revel, and we aren't inviting you, either.

· 18 ·

For you're a pain when you're present, and beloved
when you're away.

(1207-208)[5]

The separating power of space can be marked with
various activities; by racing through it, for example, as
Atalanta does when she puts miles between herself and
her suitors:

. . . ὥς ποτέ φασιν
Ἰασίου κούρην παρθένον Ἰασίην,
ὡραίην περ ἐοῦσαν, ἀναινομένην γάμον ἀνδρῶν
φεύγειν· ζωσαμένη δ᾽ ἔργ᾽ ἀτέλεστα τέλει
πατρὸς νοσφισθεῖσα δόμων ξανθὴ Ἀταλάντη·
ᾤχετο δ᾽ ὑψηλὰς ἐς κορυφὰς ὀρέων
φεύγουσ᾽. . . .

. . . as they say once
the daughter of Iasios fled young Hippomenes
and said No to marriage, although she was ripe.
But she girded herself to achieve the impossible.
Leaving behind her the house of her father,
lighthaired Atalanta,
gone to the high tops of mountains
in flight. . . .

(Theognis 1287-93)

The Trojan War and a long tradition of erotic quests represent the other side (the lover's) of this stereotypical activity. Pursuit and flight are a *topos* of Greek erotic poetry and iconography from the archaic period onward. It
is noteworthy that, within such conventional scenes, the
moment of ideal desire on which vase-painters as well as
poets are inclined to focus is not the moment of the *coup
de foudre*, not the moment when the beloved's arms open

[5] The text is that of Carrière 1962, against West 1966, whose wan
harpaleos (for the codices' *argaleos*, after Bergk) reduces a finely agi-
tated chiasmus to little.

to the lover, not the moment when the two unite in happiness. What is pictured is the moment when the beloved turns and runs. The verbs *pheugein* ('to flee') and *diōkein* ('to pursue') are a fixed item in the technical erotic vocabulary of the poets, several of whom admit that they prefer pursuit to capture. "There is a certain exquisite pleasure in the wavering of the balance" Theognis says of such erotic tension (1372). Kallimachos characterizes his own eros as a perverse hunter "bypassing game that lies available, for it knows only to pursue what flees" (*Epigrammata* 31.5-6).

Lovers who do not wish to run may stand and throw: an apple is the traditional missile in declarations of love (e.g., Ar. *Nub.* 997). The lover's ball, or *sphaira*, is another conventional mechanism of seduction, so often tossed as a love challenge (e.g., Anakreon 358 *PMG; Anth. Pal.* 5.214, 6.280) that it came to emblematize the god himself, as Eros Ballplayer, in later verse (Ap. Rhod. 3.132-41). The glance of the eye can be an equally potent projectile. The poets call upon a vocabulary of innuendo that ranges from the "slantwise stare" of a flirting Thracian filly (Anakreon 417 *PMG*) to Astymeloisa's glance "more melting than sleep or death" (Alkman 3.61-62 *PMG*) and the limb-dissolving gaze of Eros himself "down from underneath blue eyelids" (Ibykos 287 *PMG*).

Eyelids are important. From the eyelids may issue an erotic emotion that sets the interval between two people vibrating:

> *Aidōs* dwells upon the eyelids of sensitive people
> as does *hybris* upon the insensitive. A wise man
>   would know this.
>   (Stob. *Flor.* 4.230M)

Aidōs ('shamefastness') is a sort of voltage of decorum discharged between two people approaching one another for the crisis of human contact, an instinctive and

mutual sensitivity to the boundary between them. It is
the shame suitably felt by a suppliant at the hearth (e.g.,
Od. 17.578), a guest before his host (e.g., *Od.* 8.544),
youth making way for old age (e.g., Soph. *OC* 247), as
well as the shared shyness that radiates between lover
and beloved (e.g., Pind. *Pyth.* 9.9-13). The proverbial
residence of *aidōs* upon sensitive eyelids is a way of saying that *aidōs* exploits the power of the glance by with-
holding it, and also that one must watch one's feet to
avoid the misstep called *hybris*. In erotic contexts *aidōs*
can demarcate like a third presence, as in a fragment of
Sappho that records the overture of a man to a woman:

θέλω τί τ᾿ εἴπην, ἀλλά με κωλύει αἴδως. . . .

I want to say something to you, but *aidos* prevents
me. . . .

(*LP*, fr. 137.1-2)

The static electricity of erotic "shame" is a very dis-
creet way of marking that two are not one. More vul-
garly, *aidōs* may materialize as an object or a gesture.
Here again the conventions of Greek vase-painting assist
our understanding of poetic nuances. Erotic scenes on
vases offer clear evidence that eros deferred or obstructed, rather than eros triumphant, is the favored subject. Pederastic vases frequently depict the following moment: a man touches a boy on chin and genitals (the
customary gesture of erotic invitation), while the boy responds with the (equally customary) gesture of dissua-
sion, right arm turning away the man's hand from his
chin. One vase has the inscribed dialogue: "Let me!"
"Stop it!" This image of the two courtship gestures inter-
secting at a moment of impasse seems to summarize
erotic experience for these painters. "Eros is often
sweeter when he is being difficult" says a Hellenistic poet
(*Anth. Pal.* 12.153). Heterosexual scenes, in Greek poetry as well as visual art, make significant use of the

woman's veil. A chaste wife like Penelope in Homer's *Odyssey* "holds her veil up on either side of her face" (16.416, 18.210) when confronting suitors, while Medea's decision to abandon chastity for Jason is indicated by "holding her veil aside" (Ap. Rhod. 3.444-45). Plato takes over the motif of veiling in an erotic scenario between Sokrates and Alkibiades in his *Symposium*. Alkibiades is recounting the frustrations of his love affair with Sokrates. The affair is getting nowhere because Sokrates steadfastly fails to respond to Alkibiades' beauty. Even when they sleep in the same bed, nothing happens. A cloak comes between them:

Ἐγὼ μὲν δὴ ταῦτα ἀκούσας τε καὶ εἰπών, καὶ ἀφεὶς ὥσπερ βέλη, τετρῶσθαι αὐτὸν ᾤμην· καὶ ἀναστάς γε, οὐδ᾽ ἐπιτρέψας τούτῳ εἰπεῖν οὐδὲν ἔτι, ἀμφιέσας τὸ ἱμάτιον τὸ ἐμαυτοῦ τοῦτον—καὶ γὰρ ἦν χειμών—ὑπὸ τὸν τρίβωνα κατακλινεὶς τὸν τουτουί, περιβαλὼν τὼ χεῖρε τούτῳ τῷ δαιμονίῳ ὡς ἀληθῶς καὶ θαυμαστῷ, κατεκείμην τὴν νύκτα ὅλην. καὶ οὐδὲ ταῦτα αὖ, ὦ Σώκρατες, ἐρεῖς ὅτι ψεύδομαι. ποιήσαντος δὲ δὴ ταῦτα ἐμοῦ οὗτος τοσοῦτον περιεγένετό τε καὶ κατεφρόνησεν καὶ κατεγέλασεν τῆς ἐμῆς ὥρας καὶ ὕβρισεν—καὶ περὶ ἐκεῖνό γε ᾤμην τὶ εἶναι, ὦ ἄνδρες δικασταί· δικασταὶ γάρ ἐστε τῆς Σωκράτους ὑπερηφανίας—εὖ γὰρ ἴστε μὰ θεούς, μὰ θεάς, οὐδὲν περιττότερον καταδεδαρθηκὼς ἀνέστην μετὰ Σωκράτους, ἢ εἰ μετὰ πατρὸς καθηῦδον ἢ ἀδελφοῦ πρεσβυτέρου.

Well, after I had exchanged these words with him . . . I got up and, without permitting the man to say anything more, wrapped my own cloak around him—it was winter—stretched out under his threadbare coat, wound my two arms around this genuinely miraculous, amazing man and lay there all night long. . . . And when I had done this, he so scorned and disdained it, and laughed at my beauty

· 22 ·

and made light of the very thing I thought was a big
deal . . . that when I rose I had no more "slept with"
Sokrates than if I had lain down with my father or
elder brother.   (219b-c)

There are two garments in this scene and the way Alkibiades uses them is a concrete symbol of his own contradictory desire: he first wraps Sokrates up in his own
cloak (because it is a cold winter night) then throws Sokrates' old coat over himself and lies on the bed, embracing the bundled-up object of his desire, until morning.
Both the gesture of embrace and the gesture of separation
are Alkibiades' own. Eros is lack: Alkibiades reifies the
lover's guiding principle almost as self-consciously as
Tristan, who places a drawn sword between himself and
Iseult when they lie down to sleep in the forest.

This principle is reified also in the social attitudes that
surround a lover. A society, like our own, for example,
that sets a high value on both the chastity and the prolif-
icacy of the female, will assign to the beloved the role of
seductive unattainability. A titillating triangle comes into
play between the lover, the bad girl who attracts him and
the good girl who honours him by saying no. Familiar
with such double standards ourselves, we may look to
fifth-century Athens for their archetype. Double standards are a topic of conversation in Plato's *Symposium*,
where Pausanias describes the contradictory ethic en-
joined upon homosexual lovers by Athenian social convention (183c-85c). Upper-class mores encouraged men
to fall in love with and lay suit to beautiful boys while at
the same time commending boys who spurned such at-
tentions. "It is no simple thing" to understand or to practice such an ethic, says Pausanias (183d) and he attaches
to it the interesting label *poikilos nomos*. Let us consider
what Pausanias means.

The phrase *poikilos nomos* sums up the problem of
erotic ambivalence. *Nomos* means 'law,' 'custom,' or

'convention' and refers to the code of conduct for Athenian lovers and their boys in aristocratic circles of the time. *Poikilos* is an adjective applicable to anything variegated, complex or shifting, for example, a 'dappled' fawn, a 'spangled' wing, an 'intricately wrought' metal, a 'complicated' labyrinth, an 'abstruse' mind, a 'subtle' lie, a 'devious' double-entendre. *Nomos* implies something fixed firm in conventional sentiment and behavior; *poikilos* refers to what scintillates with change and ambiguity. The phrase verges on oxymoron; or at least the relation between noun and adjective is a richly devious one. The Athenian *nomos* is *poikilos* in that it recommends an ambivalent code of behavior (lovers should chase beloveds yet beloveds should not be caught). But the *nomos* is also *poikilos* in that it applies to a phenomenon whose essence and loveliness is *in* its ambivalence. This erotic code is a social expression of the division within a lover's heart. Double standards of behavior reflect double or contradictory pressures within erotic emotion itself.

Even more blatant was the legitimation given erotic ambivalence by Cretan society with its peculiar custom of *harpagmos*, a ritual homosexual rape of boys by their lovers. The rape began with a conventional gift-exchange and ended with the rapist carrying off his beloved on horseback for a two-month sojourn in hiding. As the couple rode away, the boy's family and friends would stand around uttering token cries of distress: "If the man is equal to or superior to the boy, people follow and resist the rape only enough to satisfy the law but are really glad . . ." confides the fourth-century historian Ephoros (*FGrH* F148). The roles in this erotic set piece are conventional. Legitimate marriage rites throughout the Greek world adopted much of the same imagery and attitude. Mock abduction of the bride formed the central action of the Spartan wedding ceremony and a similar rite may have been practiced at Lokri and other Greek states, including Athens (Sirvinou-Inwood 1973, 12-21). Painters who depict such rites on vases make clear by iconographic details of posture, gesture and facial expression that a scene of resistance and tension is being represented, not a happy and harmonious elopement. The abducting bridegroom may hold his bride diagonally across his body as he mounts the wedding chariot; the bride expresses unwillingness by various startled gestures of the left hand and arm; frequently she is seen pulling her veil across her face with one hand in the symbolic gesture of female *aidōs* (Jenkins, 1983, 137-45). It should be emphasized that these paintings, although evocative of mythical prototypes like the rape of Persephone, are not in themselves to be interpreted as mythical scenes but as ideal representations of normal wedding rites, bristling with ambiguities as such rituals do in many cultures. Anthropologists explain the ambiguities from many different angles, for marriage finds analogies in war, initiation, death or a combination of these in various societies. From beneath these social and religious layers, however, a fundamental emotional fact exerts its shaping pressure on iconography and ritual concept: eros. Such societal and aesthetic sanction given at once to lover's pursuit and beloved's flight has its image on Greek vases as a moment of impasse in the ritual of courtship, its conceptual ground in the traditionally bittersweet character of desire. *Odi et amo* intersect; there is the core and symbol of eros, in the space across which desire reaches.

The Reach

Lest thou thy love and hate and me undoe,
To let mee live, O love and hate mee too.

John Donne, "The Prohibition"

⌠ A space must be maintained or desire ends. Sappho re-
constructs the space of desire in a poem that is like a
small, perfect photograph of the erotic dilemma. The
poem is thought to be an epithalamium (or part of an epithalamium) because the ancient rhetorician Himerios
alluded to it in the course of a discussion of weddings,
saying:

> It was Sappho who likened a girl to an apple . . . and
> compared a bridegroom to Achilles. (*Orationes*
> 9.16)

We cannot certainly say whether Sappho composed this
poem for a wedding and intended it as praise of a bride,
but its overt subject remains clear and coherent. It is a
poem about desire. Both its content and its form consist
in an act of reaching:

οἶον τὸ γλυκύμαλον ἐρεύθεται ἄκρῳ ἐπ᾽ ὔσδῳ,
ἄκρον ἐπ᾽ ἀκροτάτῳ, λελάθοντο δὲ μαλοδρόπηες,
οὐ μὰν ἐκλελάθοντ᾽, ἀλλ᾽ οὐκ ἐδύναντ᾽ ἐπίκεσθαι

As a sweet apple turns red on a high branch,
high on the highest branch and the applepickers
    forgot—
well, no they didn't forget—were not able to reach
    . . .

(*LP*, fr. 105a)

The poem is incomplete, perfectly. There is one sentence, which has no principal verb or principal subject because the sentence never arrives at its main clause. It is one simile, whose point remains elusive since the *comparandum* never appears. It may be from an epithalamium, but it seems precarious to say so in the absence of the wedding party. If there is a bride, she stays inaccessible. It is her inaccessibility that is present. As the object of comparison suspended in line 1, it exerts a powerful attraction, both grammatical and erotic, on all that follows; but completion is not achieved—grammatical or erotic. Desiring hands close on empty air in the final infinitive, while the apple of their eye dangles perpetually inviolate two lines above.

The action of the poem occurs in present indicative verbs that attain, with the last word, infinite disappointment. This final falling short is gently, repeatedly prepared by what comes before. The three lines of the poem follow the poet's mind on a trajectory through perception to judgment, a trajectory in which both the perception (of the apple) and the judgment (of why it is where it is) suffer self-correction. As the poet's eye reaches up to locate the apple ("on a high branch"), that location is made more exact ("high on the highest branch") and more remote. As the poet's interpretation reaches to explain the apple ("and the applepickers forgot"), that explanation is emended in stride ("well, no they didn't forget—were unable to reach"). Each line launches an impression that is at once modified, then launched again. Second thoughts grow out of initial misapprehensions, and this mental action is reflected in the sounds of the words as the anaphoric syllables reach after one another from verse to verse (*akrō . . . akron . . . akrotatō lelathonto . . . eklelathont'*). This motion is corroborated in the rhythm of the verse: dactyls (in lines 1 and 2) slow and elongate to spondees (in line 3) as the apple begins to look farther and farther away.

Each verse, we should also note, applies corrective

measures to its own units of sound. The first verse contains two examples of a metrical procedure called 'correption.' Correption is a licence permitted to dactylic hexameter whereby a long vowel or diphthong is shortened but allowed to remain in hiatus before a following vowel. Here the two correptions occur in close succession (*-tai akrō ep-*) and make the verse seem crowded with sounds that move and rustle against one another, as the tree is thick with branches over which your eye climbs steadily to the topmost one. Lines 2 and 3 make use of a different corrective device: elision. Elision is a brusquer approach to the metrical problem of hiatus; it simply expels the first vowel. Elision occurs once in the second line (*ep' ak-*) and three times in the third verse (*-thont' all' ouk edunant' ep-*). Both correption and elision may be regarded as tactics to restrain a unit of sound from reaching beyond its proper position in the rhythm. The tactics differ in permissiveness, for the former partially concedes, while the latter entirely curtails, the reach. (Or one might think of correption as a sort of metrical décolletage, in contrast to elision, which bundles the too tempting vowel quite out of sight.) One gets the sense, as the poem proceeds, of a gradually imposed constraint. The reaching action of desire is attempted again and again in different ways through the different lines; with each line it becomes clearer that the reach will not succeed. The triple elision of line 3 is conspicuous. Lines 1 and 2 permit the poet's eye a comparatively uninhibited ascent to the topmost apple. Line 3 crops the apple-pickers' hands in midair.

There are five elisions in the poems, of which three affect the preposition *epi*. This word deserves our closer attention for it is crucial to the etymology and morphology of the poem. *Epi* is a preposition expressing motion to, toward, for, in quest of, reaching after. The action of this ardent preposition shapes the poem on every level. In its sounds, in its rythmic effects, in its process of thought, in its narrative content (and in its external occasion, if these lines are from an epithalamium) this poem acts out the experience of eros. It is a compound experience, both *gluku* and *pikron*: Sappho begins with a sweet apple and ends in infinite hunger. From her inchoate little poem we learn several things about eros. The reach of desire is defined in action: beautiful (in its object), foiled (in its attempt), endless (in time).

Finding the Edge

Eros is an issue of boundaries. He exists because certain boundaries do. In the interval between reach and grasp, between glance and counterglance, between 'I love you' and 'I love you too,' the absent presence of desire comes alive. But the boundaries of time and glance and I love you are only aftershocks of the main, inevitable boundary that creates Eros: the boundary of flesh and self between you and me. And it is only, suddenly, at the moment when I would dissolve that boundary, I realize I never can.

Infants begin to see by noticing the edges of things. How do they know an edge is an edge? By passionately wanting it not to be. The experience of eros as lack alerts a person to the boundaries of himself, of other people, of things in general. It is the edge separating my tongue from the taste for which it longs that teaches me what an edge is. Like Sappho's adjective *glukupikron*, the moment of desire is one that defies proper edge, being a compound of opposites forced together at pressure. Pleasure and pain at once register upon the lover, inasmuch as the desirability of the love object derives, in part, from its lack. To whom is it lacking? To the lover. If we follow the trajectory of eros we consistently find it tracing out this same route: it moves out from the lover toward the beloved, then ricochets back to the lover himself and the hole in him, unnoticed before. Who is the real subject of most love poems? Not the beloved. It is that hole.

When I desire you a part of me is gone: my want of you

· 30 ·

partakes of me. So reasons the lover at the edge of eros. The presence of want awakens in him nostalgia for wholeness. His thoughts turn toward questions of personal identity: he must recover and reincorporate what is gone if he is to be a complete person. The *locus classicus* for this view of desire is the speech of Aristophanes in Plato's *Symposium*. Here Aristophanes accounts for the nature of human eros by means of a fantastic anthropology (189d-93d). Human beings were originally round organisms, each composed of two people joined together as one perfect sphere. These rolled about everywhere and were exceedingly happy. But the spherical creatures grew overambitious, thinking to roll right up to Olympus, so Zeus chopped each of them in two. As a result everyone must now go through life in search of the one and only other person who can round him out again. "Sliced in two like a flatfish," says Aristophanes, "each of us is perpetually hunting for the matching half of himself" (191d).

Most people find something disturbingly lucid and true in Aristophanes' image of lovers as people cut in half. All desire is for a part of oneself gone missing, or so it feels to the person in love. Aristophanes' myth justifies that feeling, in typical Greek fashion, by blaming the whole situation on Zeus. But Aristophanes is a comic poet. We might look, for a more serious exegesis, to more serious lovers. A feature of their reasoning will at once strike us. It is outrageous.

Logic at the Edge

... with one impulse of the heart we only just grazed it—
and sighing left the first fruits of our spirit there and came
back to the sound of our human tongue where words have
beginnings and endings.

Augustine, *Confessions* 9.10

When I desire you a part of me is gone: your lack is my
lack. I would not be in want of you unless you had par-
taken of me, the lover reasons. "A hole is being gnawed
in [my] vitals" says Sappho (*LP*, fr. 96.16-17). "You
have snatched the lungs out of my chest" (West, *IEG*
191) and "pierced me right through the bones" (193)
says Archilochos. "You have worn me down" (Alkman
1.77 *PMG*), "grated me away" (Ar., *Eccl.* 956), "de-
voured my flesh" (Ar., *Ran.* 66), "sucked my blood"
(Theokritos 2.55), "mowed off my genitals" (?Archilo-
chos, West, *IEG* 99.21), "stolen my reasoning mind"
(Theognis 1271). Eros is expropriation. He robs the
body of limbs, substance, integrity and leaves the lover,
essentially, less. This attitude toward love is grounded
for the Greeks in oldest mythical tradition: Hesiod describes in his *Theogony* how castration gave birth to the
goddess Aphrodite, born from the foam around Oura-
nos' severed genitals (189-200). Love does not happen
without loss of vital self. The lover is the loser. Or so he
reckons.

But his reckoning involves a quick and artful shift.
Reaching for an object that proves to be outside and be-

· 32 ·

yond himself, the lover is provoked to notice that self and
its limits. From a new vantage point, which we might call
self-consciousness, he looks back and sees a hole. Where
does that hole come from? It comes from the lover's clas-
sificatory process. Desire for an object *that he never
knew he lacked* is defined, by a shift of distance, as desire
for a necessary part of himself. Not a new acquisition but
something that was always, properly, *his*. Two lacks become one.

The shifty logic of the lover unfolds naturally from his
ruses of desire. We have seen how lovers, like Sappho in
fragment 31, recognize Eros as a sweetness made out of
absence and pain. The recognition calls into play various
tactics of triangulation, various ways of keeping the
space of desire open and electric. To think about one's
own tactics is always a tricky business. The exegesis
measures out three angles: the lover himself, the beloved,
the lover redefined as incomplete without the beloved.
But this trigonometry is a trick. The lover's next move is
to collapse the triangle into a two-sided figure and treat
the two sides as one circle. 'Seeing my hole, I know my
whole' he says to himself. His own reasoning process
suspends him between the two terms of this pun.

It seems impossible to talk or reason about erotic lack
without falling into this punning language. Consider, for
example, Plato's *Lysis*. In this dialogue Sokrates is attempting to define the Greek word *philos*, which means
both 'loving' and 'loved,' both 'friendly' and 'dear.' He
takes up the question whether the desire to love or be-
friend something is ever separable from lack of it. His interlocutors are led to acknowledge that all desire is longing for that which *properly belongs to the desirer* but has
been lost or taken away somehow—no one says how
(221e-22a). Puns flash as the reasoning quickens. This
part of the discussion depends upon an adroit use of the
Greek word *oikeios*, which means both 'suitable, related,

akin to myself' and 'belonging to me, properly *mine*.' So Sokrates addresses the two boys who are his interlocutors and says:

. . . Τοῦ οἰκείου δή, ὡς ἔοικεν, ὅ τε ἔρως καὶ ἡ φιλία καὶ ἡ ἐπιθυμία τυγχάνει οὖσα, ὡς φαίνεται, ὦ Με-νέξενέ τε καὶ Λύσι.—Συνεφάτην.—Ὑμεῖς ἄρα εἰ φίλοι ἐστὸν ἀλλήλοις, φύσει πῃ οἰκεῖοί ἐσθ᾽ ὑμῖν αὐτοῖς.

. . . Desire and love and longing are directed at that which is akin to oneself [*tou oikeiou*], it seems. So if you two are loving friends [*philoi*] of one another then in some natural way you belong to one another [*oikeioi esth'*]. (221e)

It is profoundly unjust of Sokrates to slip from one meaning of *oikeios* to another, as if it were the same thing to recognize in someone else a kindred soul and to claim that soul as your own possession, as if it were perfectly acceptable in love to blur the distinction between yourself and the one you love. All the lover's reasoning and hopes of happiness are built upon this injustice, this claim, this blurred distinction. So his thought process is continually moving and searching through the borderland of language where puns occur. What is the lover searching for there?

A pun is a figure of language that depends on similarity of sound and disparity of meaning. It matches two sounds that fit perfectly together as aural shapes yet stand insistently, provocatively apart in sense. You perceive homophony and at the same time see the semantic space that separates the two words. Sameness is projected onto difference in a kind of stereoscopy. There is something irresistible in that. Puns appear in all literatures, are apparently as old as language and unfailingly fascinate us. Why? If we had the answer to this question we would know more clearly what the lover is searching

for as he moves and reasons through the borderlands of
his desire.

We do not yet have an answer. Nonetheless we should
pay attention to the punning character of the lover's
logic: its structure and its irresistibility have something
important to tell us about desire, and about the lover's
search. We have seen how Sokrates makes use of punning
language to slip from one sense of *oikeios* ('kindred') to
another sense ('mine') when in the *Lysis* he is discussing
eros as lack. Sokrates makes no attempt to conceal his
wordplay here; indeed, he draws attention to it with an
uncommon grammatical usage. He deliberately mixes up
reciprocal and reflexive pronouns when he addresses the
two *philoi*, Lysis and Menexenos. That is, when he says
to them ". . . you belong to one another" (221e6) he uses
a word for 'one another' that more commonly means
'yourselves' (*hautois*). Sokrates is playing, through
words, upon the desires of the young lovers before him.
Mix-up of self and other is much more easily achieved in
language than in life, but somewhat the same effrontery
is involved. Like eros, puns flout the edges of things.
Their power to allure and alarm derives from this.
Within a pun you see the possibility of grasping a *better*
truth, a *truer* meaning, than is available from the separate senses of either word. But the glimpse of that enhanced meaning, which flashes past in a pun, is a painful
thing. For it is inseparable from your conviction of its impossibility. Words do have edges. So do you.

The punning logic of the lover is an important piece of
cogitation. The lover's puns show the outline of what he
learns, in a flash, from the experience of eros— a vivid
lesson about his own being. When he inhales Eros, there
appears within him a sudden vision of a different self,
perhaps a better self, compounded of his own being and
that of his beloved. Touched to life by erotic accident,
this enlargement of self is a complex and unnerving oc-
currence. All too easily it becomes ridiculous, as we see

for example when Aristophanes takes the typical lover's fantasy to its logical, circular conclusion in his myth of round people. But at the same time a sensation of serious truth accompanies the lover's vision of himself. There is something uniquely convincing about the perceptions that occur to you when you are in love. They seem truer than other perceptions, and more truly your *own*, won from reality at personal cost. Greatest certainty is felt about the beloved as necessary complement to you. Your powers of imagination connive at this vision, calling up possibilities from beyond the actual. All at once a self never known before, which now strikes you as the true one, is coming into focus. A gust of godlikeness may pass through you and for an instant a great many things look knowable, possible and present. Then the edge asserts itself. You are not a god. You are not that enlarged self. Indeed, you are not even a whole self, as you now see. Your new knowledge of possibilities is also a knowledge of what is lacking in the actual.

We might look, for purposes of comparison, at how this insight takes shape within the mind of a modern lover. In her novel *The Waves*, Virginia Woolf describes a young man named Neville watching his beloved Bernard approach him from across a garden:

> Something now leaves me; something goes from me to meet that figure who is coming, and assures me that I know him before I see who it is. How curiously one is changed by the addition, even at a distance, of a friend. How useful an office one's friends perform when they recall us. Yet how painful to be recalled, to be mitigated, to have one's self adulterated, mixed up, become part of another. As he approaches I become not myself but Neville mixed with somebody—with whom?—with Bernard? Yes, it is Bernard, and it is to Bernard that I shall put the question, Who am I? (83)

Neville is less alarmed by the hole in him than are the Greek lyric poets when they record the depradations of eros. And, unlike Sokrates, Neville does not resort to puns to account for his mixed-up condition. He simply watches it happen and measures off its three angles: desire moves out from Neville himself, ricochets off Bernard, and bends back to Neville—but not the same Neville. "I become not myself but Neville mixed with somebody." The piece of himself that goes out to Bernard makes Bernard immediately familiar "even before I see who it is." As Sokrates would say, it makes Bernard *oikeios*. Even so, Neville goes on to appraise the experience as an ambivalent one, both "useful" and "painful." As in the Greek poets, its pain arises at that edge where the self is adulterated and bitter verges alarmingly on sweet. Eros' ambivalence unfolds directly from this power to 'mix up' the self. The lover helplessly admits that it feels both good and bad to be mixed up, but is then driven back upon the question 'Once I have been mixed up in this way, who am I?' Desire *changes* the lover. "How curiously": he feels the change happen but has no ready categories to assess it. The change gives him a glimpse of a self he never knew before.

Some such glimpse may be the mechanism that originally shapes a notion of 'self' in each of us, according to some analyses. Freudian theory traces this notion to a fundamental decision of love and hate, somewhat like the ambivalent condition of the lover, that splits our souls and forms our personality. There is at the beginning of life, in the Freudian view, no awareness of objects as distinct from one's own body. The distinction between self and not-self is made by the decision to claim all that the ego likes as 'mine' and to reject all that the ego dislikes as 'not mine.' Divided, we learn where our selves end and the world begins. Self-taught, we love what we can make our own and hate what remains other.

Historians of the Greek psyche, notably Bruno Snell,

have adapted Freud's ontogenetic picture to account for the rise of individualism in Greek society during the archaic and early classical periods. In the view of Snell, the first formation in Greek society of a self-conscious and self-controlled human personality, aware of itself as an organic whole distinct from other personalities and from the world around it, can be traced to a moment of emotional ambivalence that splits the soul. Sappho's adjective *glukupikron* signals that moment. It is a revolution in human self-awareness that Snell calls "the discovery of the mind." Blocked eros is its trigger. Its consequence is the consolidation of a 'self':

> The love which has its course barred, and fails to reach its fulfilment acquires a particularly strong hold over the human heart. The sparks of a vital desire burst into flame at the very moment when the desire is blocked in its path. It is the obstruction which makes the wholly personal feelings conscious. . . . [the frustrated lover] seeks the cause in his own personality. (1953, 53)

Snell's is a sensational thesis and has provoked excitement, wide dissent and ongoing controversy. No resolution of the questions of history and historiography involved is available, but Snell's insight about the importance of bittersweet love in our lives in a powerful one, appealing to the common experience of many lovers. Neville, for example, seems to come round to the same conclusion, as he ponders his love for Bernard, in *The Waves*: "To be contracted by another person into a single being—how strange"(80).

Losing the Edge

The self forms at the edge of desire, and a science of self arises in the effort to leave that self behind. But more than one response is possible to the acute awareness of self that ensues from the reach of desire. Neville conceives it as a "contraction" of the self upon itself and finds it merely strange. "How curiously one is changed," he muses. He does not appear to hate the change, nor to relish it. Nietzsche, on the other hand, is delighted: "One seems to oneself transfigured, stronger, richer, more complete; one *is* more complete. . . . It is not merely that it changes the feeling of values; the lover *is* worth more" (1967, 426). It is not uncommon in love to experience this heightened sense of one's own personality ('I am more myself than ever before!' the lover feels) and to rejoice in it, as Nietzsche does. The Greek lyric poets do not so rejoice.

Change of self is loss of self to these poets. Their metaphors for the experience are metaphors of war, disease and bodily dissolution. These metaphors assume a dynamic of assault and resistance. Extreme sensual tension between the self and its environment is the poets' focus, and a particular image of that tension predominates. In Greek lyric poetry, eros is an experience of melting. The god of desire himself is traditionally called "melter of limbs" (Sappho, *LP*, fr. 130; Archilochos, West, *IEG* 196). His glance is "more melting than sleep or death" (Alkman 3 *PMG*). The lover whom he victimizes is a piece of wax, (Pindar, Snell-Maehler, fr. 123) dissolving at his touch. Is melting a good thing? That remains am-

bivalent. The image implies something sensually delicious, yet anxiety and confusion often attend it. Viscosity
is an experience that repels in its own right, in the view
of Jean-Paul Sartre. His remarks on the phenomenon
stickiness may cast some light on the ancient attitude toward love:

> An infant plunging its hands into a jar of honey is
> instantly involved in contemplating the formal
> properties of solids and liquids and the essential re-
> lation between the subjective experiencing self and
> the experienced world. The viscous is a state half-
> way between solid and liquid. It is like a cross-sec-
> tion in a process of change. It is unstable but it does
> not flow. It is soft, yielding, and compressible. Its
> stickiness is a trap, it clings like a leech; it attacks the
> boundary between myself and it. Long columns fall-
> ing off my fingers suggest my own substance flowing
> into the pool of stickiness. Plunging into water gives
> a different impression; I remain a solid. But to touch
> stickiness is to risk diluting myself into viscosity.
> Stickiness is clinging, like a too possessive dog or
> mistress. (1956, 606-607)

Sartre's high-pitched ("it clings like a leech") and all but
irrational ("stickiness is a trap") dismay at self-dilution
has its analog in the ancient poets' response to eros.
Nonetheless, Sartre believes that something important
can be learned from stickiness, as from a dogged mistress, about the properties of matter and the interrelation
between self and other things. In experiencing and artic-
ulating the melting threat of eros, the Greek poets are
presumably also learning something about their own
bounded selves through the effort to resist dissolution of
those bounds in erotic emotion. The physiology that they
posit for the erotic experience is one which assumes eros
to be hostile in intention and detrimental in effect.
Alongside melting we might cite metaphors of piercing,

crushing, bridling, roasting, stinging, biting, grating, cropping, poisoning, singeing and grinding to a powder, all of which are used of eros by the poets, giving a cumulative impression of intense concern for the integrity and control of one's own body. The lover learns as he loses it to value the bounded entity of himself.

A crisis of contact, like the child's encounter with honey in Sartre's example, evokes this learning experience. Nowhere in the Western tradition is that crisis so vividly recorded as in Greek lyric verse, and literary historians like Bruno Snell claim primacy for the archaic age on the basis of this evidence. It is unfortunate that, in making this claim, Snell neglects an aspect of ancient experience that cuts straight across his record and might have furnished compelling testimony for his thesis, namely the phenomenon of alphabetic literacy. Reading and writing change people and change societies. It is not always easy to see how nor to trace out the subtle map of cause and effect that links such changes to their context. But we should make an effort to do so. There is an important, unanswerable question here. Is it a matter of coincidence that the poets who invented Eros, making of him a divinity and a literary obsession, were also the first authors in our tradition to leave us their poems in written form? To put the question more pungently, what is erotic about alphabetization? This may seem not so much an unanswerable as a foolish question, at first, but let us look closer into the selves of the first writers. Selves are crucial to writers.

Whether or not it seems fair to ascribe to the archaic poets a "discovery of mind" such as Snell outlines, undeniable evidence remains, in the preserved fragments of their verses, of a sensibility acutely tuned to the vulnerability of the physical body and of the emotions or spirit within it. Such a sensibility is not given voice in the poetry we have from before this period. Perhaps this is due to an accident of technology. Lyric poetry and the sensibility typical of it begin for us with Archilochos because his poems came to be written down, we do not know how or why, sometime in the seventh or sixth century B.C. Perhaps there were many Archilochoses before him composing oral lyrics about the depradations of Eros. Nonetheless, the fact that Archilochos and his lyric successors derive from a written tradition marks in itself a decisive difference between them and whatever was before, not just because it gives us their texts but because it cues us to certain radically new conditions of life and mind within which they were operating. Oral cultures and literate cultures do not think, perceive or fall in love in the same way.

The archaic age was in general a time of change, unrest and reordering. In politics with the rise of the *polis*, in economics with the invention of coinage, in poetics with the study by lyric poets of precise moments in personal life, and in communications technology with the introduction of the Phoenician alphabet to Greece, this period may be seen as one of contraction and focus: contraction of large structures into smaller units, focus upon definition of those units. The phenomenon of alphabetization and the beginning of the spread of literacy throughout Greek society was perhaps the most dramatic of the innovations with which seventh- and sixth-century Greeks had to cope. The alphabet must have reached the Aegean in the course of trade by the second half of the eighth century, date of the earliest Greek examples yet found. Its dissemination was slow and its consequences are still being analyzed by scholars.[6] What difference does literacy make?

[6] Eric A. Havelock broke this ground in 1963 with his *Preface to Plato*, and he has continued to pursue the matter ever since; a bibliography is assembled in his recent collection, *The Literate Revolution in Greece and Its Cultural Consequences* (1982). See also Havelock and Hershbell 1978; Cole 1981; Davison 1962; Finnegan 1977; Goody 1968 and 1977; Graff 1981; Harvey 1978; Innis 1951; Johnston 1983; Knox 1968; Pomeroy 1977; Stolz and Shannon 1976; Svenbro 1976; Turner 1952.

Most obviously, the introduction of writing revolutionizes techniques of literary composition. Denys Page summarizes the practical details of the change as follows:

> The principal characteristic of the pre-alphabetic method of poetic composition is dependence on a traditional stock of memorised formulas which, however flexible and receptive of additions and modifications, dictate in large measure not only the form but also the matter of poetry. The use of writing enabled the poet to make the word, rather than the phrase, the unit of composition; it assisted him to express ideas and describe events outside the traditional range; it gave him time to prepare his work in advance of publication, to pre-meditate more easily and at greater leisure what he should write, and to alter what he had written. (Fondation Hardt 1963, 119)

At the same time, a more private revolution is set in process by the phenomenon of alphabetization. As the audio-tactile world of the oral culture is transformed into a world of words on paper where vision is the principal conveyor of information, a reorientation of perceptual abilities begins to take place within the individual.

An individual who lives in an oral culture uses his senses differently than one who lives in a literate culture, and with that different sensual deployment comes a different way of conceiving his own relations with his environment, a different conception of his body and a different conception of his self. The difference revolves around the physiological and psychological phenomenon of individual self-control. Self-control is minimally stressed in an oral milieu where most of the data important for survival and understanding are channelled into the individual through the open conduits of his senses, particularly his sense of sound, in a continuous interaction linking him with the world outside him. Complete openness to the environment is a condition of optimum awareness and alertness for such a person, and a continual fluent interchange of sensual impressions and responses between the environment and himself is the proper condition of his physical and mental life. To close his senses off from the outside world would be counterproductive to life and to thought.

When people begin to learn reading and writing, a different scenario develops. Reading and writing require focusing the mental attention upon a text by means of the visual sense. As an individual reads and writes he gradually learns to close or inhibit the input of his senses, to inhibit or control the responses of his body, so as to train energy and thought upon the written words. He resists the environment outside him by distinguishing and controlling the one inside him. This constitutes at first a laborious and painful effort for the individual, psychologists and sociologists tell us. In making the effort he becomes aware of the interior self as an entity separable from the environment and its input, controllable by his own mental action. The recognition that such controlling action is possible, and perhaps necessary, marks an important stage in ontogenetic as in phylogenetic development, a stage at which the individual personality gathers itself to resist disintegration.

If the presence or absence of literacy affects the way a person regards his own body, senses and self, that effect will significantly influence erotic life. It is in the poetry of those who were first exposed to a written alphabet and the demands of literacy that we encounter deliberate meditation upon the self, especially in the context of erotic desire. The singular intensity with which these poets insist on conceiving eros as lack may reflect, in some degree, that exposure. Literate training encourages a heightened awareness of personal physical boundaries and a sense of those boundaries as the vessel of one's self. To control the boundaries is to possess oneself. For individuals to whom self-possession has become important, the influx of a sudden, strong emotion from without cannot be an unalarming event, as it may be in an oral environment where such incursions are the normal conductors of most of the important information that a person receives. When an individual appreciates that he alone is responsible for the content and coherence of his person, an influx like eros becomes a concrete personal threat. So in the lyric poets, love is something that assaults or invades the body of the lover to wrest control of it from him, a personal struggle of will and physique between the god and his victim. The poets record this struggle from within a consciousness—perhaps new in the world—of the body as a unity of limbs, senses and self, amazed at its own vulnerability.

Archilochos at the Edge

Archilochos is the first lyric poet whose transmission to us benefited from the literate revolution. Although evidence for the chronology of both poet and alphabet is uncertain, it is most plausible that, educated in the oral tradition, he encountered the new technology of writing at some point in his career and adapted himself to it. At any rate someone, perhaps Archilochos himself, wrote down these early facts of what it feels like to be violated by Eros:

τοῖος γὰρ φιλότητος ἔρως ὑπὸ καρδίην ἐλυσθεὶς
πολλὴν κατ᾽ ἀχλὺν ὀμμάτων ἔχευεν,
κλέψας ἐκ στηθέων ἀπαλὰς φρένας.

Such a longing for love, rolling itself up under
my heart,
poured down much mist over my eyes,
filching out of my chest the soft lungs—
(West, *IEG* 191)

The first word of the poem initiates a correlation. The word *toios* is a demonstrative pronoun meaning 'such,' which properly corresponds to the relative pronoun *hoios* meaning 'as,' so that a sentence beginning *toios* expects an answering clause with *hoios* to complete the thought. The poem sets out one half of this thought, then stops. Nonetheless, it has a perfect economy, as far as it goes. Every word, sound and stress is placed for a purpose. The first verse describes eros rolled up in a ball beneath the lover's heart. The words are ordered to reflect the physiology of the moment, with *erōs* coiled dead center. A sequence of round *o* sounds (one long and five short) and bunched consonants (four pairs) gather the tension of the lover's desire into an audible pressure within him. Consonants seem to be chosen for their insinuating quality (liquids, sibilants and voiceless stops). The metrical pattern is an original mixture of dactylic and iambic units, combined in a way that imitates the action of desire: launched in an epic burst of dactyls and spondees as eros asserts its presence, the verse then dissolves into a spatter of iambs precisely at the point where desire reaches the lover's heart (*kardiēn*). The last word of the verse is a participle (*elustheis*) that has an epic past. "Rolled up in a ball under the belly of a ram" is the mode in which Odysseus escapes the Cyclops' cave (*Od.* 9.433). "Rolled up in a ball at the feet of Achilles" is the position from which Priam makes supplication for the body of his son (*Il.* 24.510). In both of these epic contexts, a posture of abject vulnerability is assumed by a genuinely powerful person, who then proceeds to work his will on the enemy confronting him. Hidden power is a traditional feature of Eros too, in poetry and art, as the innocuous *pais* whose arrows prove deadly. Archilochos places the overtone of menace quietly, setting his participle at verse-end just as it occurs in both Homeric passages.

Line 2 encloses the lover's eyes in mist from both sides. The poet's consonants soften and thicken with the fog to *l, m, n,* and *chi* sounds. These sounds are doubled and combined in a repeated pattern that comes down four times upon word-end in *n*, as if emphasizing the descent of the fog in four liquid streaks (*-lēn, -lun,- tōn, -en*). Fog is fused around the lover's eyes by the iambic rhythm of the verse, especially in the second metron (*-lun ommatōn*) where a caesura is dropped between eyes and mist.

Epic overtones of danger are again to be felt in the imagery for, in Homer, mist darkens a man's eyes at the moment of death (cf. *Il.* 20.321; 421).

With line 3 Eros completes his violation. One quick theft whistles the lungs straight out of the lover's chest. Naturally, this ends the poem: with the organ of breath gone, speech is impossible. The robbery is staged in a run of *s* sounds (five) and the verse breaks off without completing its metrical scheme (the dactylic tetrameter should be followed by an iambic metron, as in line 1). Most likely the break is a fault of transmission, rather than a factor of the poet's intention. Obviously the same explanation, namely the fragmentary condition of Archilochos' text, would account for the unfulfilled syntactical expectation set up by the correlative pronoun with which the poem begins (*toios*). On the other hand, it is a very careful poem, as far as it goes.

The *phrenes* of the lover are as far as it goes. I have translated this word 'lungs' and referred to it as 'the organ of breath.' What is breath? For the ancient Greeks, breath is consciousness, breath is perception, breath is emotion. The *phrenes* seem to be roughly identifiable with the lungs in ancient physiological theory and to contain the spirit of breath as it comes and goes (Onians 951, 66ff). The chest is regarded by the Greeks as a receptacle of sense impressions and a vehicle for each of the five senses; even vision for, in seeing, something may be breathed from the object seen and received through the eyes of the seer (e.g., Hesiod, *Scutum* 7; cf. Arist., *Sens.* 4.437b23ff). Words, thoughts, and understanding are both received and produced by the *phrenes*. So words are "winged" in Homer when they issue from the speaker and "unwinged" when they are kept in the *phrenes* unspoken (cf. *Od.* 17.57). *Phrenes* are organs of mind. As Theognis says:

Ὀφθαλμοὶ καὶ γλῶσσα καὶ οὔατα καὶ νόος ἀνδρῶν
ἐν μέσσῳ στηθέων ἐν συνετοῖς φύεται.

The eyes and tongue and ears and intelligence of a
quick-witted man
grow in the middle of his chest.
(1163-64)

Such a conception is natural among people in an oral environment (see Onians, 1951, 68). Breath is primary in-
sofar as the spoken word is. The conception has a solid
psychological and sensual basis in the daily experience of
these people. For the inhabitants of an oral society live
much more intimately blended with their surroundings
than we do. Space and the distances between things are
not of first importance; these are aspects emphasized by
the visual sense. What is vital, in a world of sound, is to
maintain continuity. This attitude pervades archaic poetry and is strikingly present as well in the perceptual theories of the ancient *physiologoi*. Empedokles' celebrated
doctrine of emanations, for example, maintains that
everything in the universe is perpetually inhaling and ex-
haling small particles called *aporrhoai* in a constant
stream (Diels, *VS*, B89). All sensations are caused by
these emanations as they are breathed in and out through
the whole skin surface of living beings (B 100.1). The
aporrhoai are mediators of perception which allow
everything in the universe to be potentially 'in touch'
with everything else (cf. Arist., *Sens.* 4.442a29). Empedokles and his contemporaries posit a universe where
the spaces between things are ignored and the interac-
tions constant. Breath is everywhere. There are no edges.

The breath of desire is Eros. Inescapable as the environment itself, with his wings he moves love in and out
of all creatures at will. The individual's total vulnerability to erotic influence is symbolized by those wings with
their multisensual power to permeate and take control of
a lover at any moment. Wings and breath transport Eros
as wings and breath convey words: an ancient analogy
between language and love is here apparent. The same irresistible sensual charm, called *peithō* in Greek, is the

mechanism of seduction in love and of persuasion in words; the same goddess (Peitho) attends upon seducer and poet. It is an analogy that makes perfect sense in the context of oral poetics, where Eros and the Muses clearly share an apparatus of sensual assault. A listener listening to an oral recitation is, as Herman Fränkel puts it, "an open force-field" (1973, 524) into whom sounds are being breathed in a continuous stream from the poet's mouth. Written words, on the other hand, do not present such an all-persuasive sensual phenomenon. Literacy desensorializes words and reader. A reader must disconnect himself from the influx of sense impressions transmitted by nose, ear, tongue and skin if he is to concentrate upon his reading. A written text separates words from one another, separates words from the environment, separates words from the reader (or writer) and separates the reader (or writer) from his environment. Separation is painful. The evidence of epigraphy shows how long it takes people to systematize word-division in writing, indicating the novelty and difficulty of this concept.[7] As separable, controllable units of meaning, each with its own visible boundary, each with its own fixed and independent use, written words project their user into isolation.

That words have edges is an insight most vivid, then, for the reader or writer of them. Heard words may have no edges, or varying edges; oral traditions may have no concept of 'word' as a fixed and bounded vocable, or may employ a flexible concept. Homer's word for 'word' (*epos*) includes the meanings 'speech,' 'tale,' 'song,' 'line of verse' or 'epic poetry as a whole.' All are breathable. The edges are irrelevant.

But edge has a clear relevance for Archilochos. His words stop in mid-breath. "A poet like Archilochos," says the historian Werner Jaeger, "has learnt how to ex-

---

[7] On word-division and related problems, see Jeffrey 1961, 43-65; Jensen 1969, 440-60; Kenyon 1899, 26-32.

press in his own personality the whole objective world and its laws, to represent them in himself" (1934–1947, 1:114). From the flesh out, it seems, Archilochos understands the law differentiating self from not-self, for Eros cuts into him just at the point where that difference lies. To know desire, to know words, is for Archilochos a matter of perceiving the edge between one entity and another. It is fashionable to say that this is true of any utterance. "In language there are only differences" Saussure (1971, 120) tells us, meaning that phonemes are characterized not by their positive qualities but by the fact that they are distinct. Yet the individuality of words must be especially felt by someone for whom written phonemes are a novelty and the edges of words newly precise.

In the next section we will observe the Greek alphabet at very close range and consider how its special genius is linked to a special sensibility about edges. But, for the moment, let us view the phenomenon of the archaic writer from a wider angle. In Archilochos and the other archaic poets we see people struck by new ways of thinking about edges—the edges of sounds, letters, words, emotions, events in time, selves. This is apparent in the way they use the materials of poetry, as well as in the things they say. Contraction and focus are the mechanism of lyric procedure. The sweep of epic narrative contracts upon a moment of emotion; the cast of characters is pared down to one ego; the poetic eye enters its subject in a single beam. The diction and meter of these poets seem to represent a systematic breakup of the huge floes of Homer's poetic system. Epic formulas of phrase and rhythm pervade lyric poetry, but they are broken apart and differently assembled in irregular shapes and joins. A poet like Archilochos shows himself master of such combinations, sharply aware of the boundary between his own and epic procedure: we saw how deftly he fastens dactylic to iambic units in the first verse of fragment 191, so that Eros hits the lover's heart just where the epic tetrameter breaks down in iambic dismay.

Breaks interrupt time and change its data. Archilochos' written texts break pieces of passing sound off from time and hold them as his own. Breaks make a person think. When I contemplate the physical spaces that articulate the letters 'I love you' in a written text, I may be led to think about other spaces, for example the space that lies between 'you' in the text and you in my life. Both of these kinds of space come into being by an act of symbolization. Both require the mind to reach out from what is present and actual to something else, something glimpsed in the imagination. In letters as in love, to imagine is to address oneself to what is not. To write words I put a symbol in place of an absent sound. To write the words 'I love you' requires a further, analogous replacement, one that is much more painful in its implication. Your absence from the syntax of my life is not a fact to be changed by written words. And it is the single fact that makes a difference to the lover, the fact that you and I are not one. Archilochos steps off the edge of that fact into extreme solitude.

Alphabetic Edge

What is so special about the Greek alphabet? Other forms of script, both pictographic and phonetic, were at hand in the ancient world, for example, Assyrian cuneiform, Egyptian hieroglyphs and various Near Eastern syllabaries. Yet the Greek alphabet came as a startling novelty and revolutionized the human ability to set down thoughts. How?

The Greeks created their alphabet by taking over the syllabic sign-system of the Phoenicians and modifying it in certain decisive ways sometime in the early eighth century B.C. It is standard to say that their chief modification amounted to "introducing the vowels." Vowels were not expressed in Phoenician writing (although it is possible certain letters were beginning to acquire some vocalic character), but from the outset the Greek alphabet had five vowels in full use (Woodhead 1981, 15). This standard description does no justice, however, to the conceptual leap that distinguishes the Greek alphabet from all other writing systems. Let us look more closely at the unique activity of symbolization made possible when the Greeks devised the original twenty-six signs of their alphabet.

A script that furnishes a true alphabet for a language is one able to symbolize the phonemes of the language exhaustively, unambiguously and economically. The first and only ancient sign system to do so was the Greek alphabet. Other phonetic systems available to the Greeks, for example, the unvocalized syllabaries of the North Semitic scripts or the vocalized syllabary known as Linear

B used by Cretans and Mycenaean Greeks prehistorically, operated on the principle of symbolizing each pronounceable sound of the language with a separate sign. Hundreds of signs were required, each representing a single syllable of vowel plus consonant. In their choice to translate sound into graphic symbol these scripts represented a decisive advance in the development of writing. But the Greek alphabet took one further notional step: it broke these pronounced units of sound apart into their acoustic components. Vowels came into being. But vowels are inconceivable without a prior, dashing innovation. For the components of every linguistic noise are two: (1) a sound (made by vibration of a column of air in the larynx or nasal cavity as it is expelled past the vocal chords); (2) the starting and stopping of the sound (by interaction of the tongue, teeth, palate, lips, and nose). The actions that start and stop sounds, which we think of as 'consonants,' can by themselves produce no sound. They are nonsounds having, as Plato said, "no voice" (*Tht.* 203b; cf. *Phlb.* 18b). The importance of these unutterable, symbolic entities called consonants is summarized by one historian this way:

> What must be stressed is that the act which created the alphabet is an idea, an act of intellect which, so far as signs for the independent consonants are concerned, is also an act of abstraction from anything an ear can hear or a voice say. For the pure consonant (t, d, k or whatever) is unpronounceable without adding to it some suggestion of vocalic breath. The Phoenician sign stood for a consonant *plus any vowel*, the vowel being supplied from context by a reader. The Greek sign, and this for the first time in the history of writing, stands for an abstraction, the isolated consonant. (Robb 1978, 31)

When we think about this remarkable invention of the Greek alphabet and think about how a human mind operates when it uses the alphabet, the remarkable operations of eros stand forward for comparison. We have already detected an ancient analogy between language and love, implicit in the conception of breath as universal conductor of seductive influences and of persuasive speech. Here at the entrance to written language and literate thinking we see that analogy revivified by the archaic writers who first ventured to record their poems. The alphabet they used is a unique instrument. Its uniqueness unfolds directly from its power to mark the edges of sound. For, as we have seen, the Greek alphabet is a phonetic system uniquely concerned to represent a certain aspect of the act of speech, namely the starting and stopping of each sound. Consonants are the crucial factor. Consonants mark the edges of sound. The erotic relevance of this is clear, for we have seen that eros is vitally alert to the edges of things and makes them felt by lovers. As eros insists upon the edges of human beings and of the spaces between them, the written consonant imposes edge on the sounds of human speech and insists on the reality of that edge, although it has its origin in the reading and writing imagination.

This analogy between the nature of eros and the genius of the Greek alphabet may seem a fanciful one to literate, modern judgments; but it seems likely our judgments in this area have been blunted by habit and indifference. We read too much, write too poorly and remember too little about the delightful discomfort of learning these skills for the first time. Think how much energy, time and emotion goes into that effort of learning: it absorbs years of your life and dominates your self-esteem; it informs much of your subsequent endeavor to grasp and communicate with the world. Think of the beauty of letters, and of how it feels to come to know them. In her autobiography Eudora Welty confesses her susceptibility to this beauty:

My love for the alphabet, which endures, grew out of reciting it but, before that, out of seeing the letters on the page. In my own story books, before I could read them for myself, I fell in love with various winding, enchanted-looking initials drawn by Walter Crane at the heads of fairy tales. In 'Once upon a time' an 'O' had a rabbit running it as a treadmill, his feet upon flowers. When the day came, years later, for me to see the Book of Kells, all the wizardry of letter, initial, and word swept over me a thousand times over, and the illumination, the gold, seemed a part of the word's beauty and holiness that had been there from the start. (1984, 9)

Eudora Welty's delight in beautifully inscribed letters is not, I think, untypical of writers. Pythagoras is said to have felt a similar aesthetic pressure:

Πυθαγόρας αὐτῶν τοῦ κάλλους ἐπεμελήθη, ἐκ τῆς κατὰ γεωμετρίαν γραμμῆς ῥυθμίσας αὐτὰ γωνίαις καὶ περιφερείαις καὶ εὐθείαις.

He took pains over the beauty of letters, forming each stroke with a geometrical rhythm of angles and curves and straight lines. (schol. Dion. Thrax, Hilgard, *Gramm. Gr.* 1.3.183)

To take pains over letters is an experience known to most of us. They are enticing, difficult shapes and you learn them by tracing the outlines again and again. So also in the ancient world children learned to write by tracing out the letter-forms, as we may judge from a passage in Plato's *Protagoras*:

ὥσπερ οἱ γραμματισταὶ τοῖς μήπω δεινοῖς γράφειν τῶν παίδων ὑπογράψαντες γραμμὰς τῇ γραφίδι οὕτω τὸ γραμματεῖον διδόασιν καὶ ἀναγκάζουσι γράφειν κατὰ τὴν ὑφήγησιν τῶν γραμμῶν,

. . . just as those who are teaching pupils not yet adept at writing draw in the strokes of the letters in

faint outline with the pen for them, then hand them
the writing tablet and have them trace over the
guidelines.... (326d)

To anyone trained in this way the edges of letters are
memorable, emotional places, and remain so.
We can see how powerfully these alphabetic outlines
struck the eyes and minds of people grappling with them
for the first time in the ancient Greek context. There are
several scenes from ancient tragedy where such an encounter is dramatized. The most extensive is a fragment
of Euripides' *Theseus*. An illiterate man is looking out to
sea and spies a ship with writing on it. He 'reads':

ἐγὼ πέφυκα γραμμάτων μὲν οὐκ ἴδρις,
μορφὰς δὲ λέξω καὶ σαφῆ τεκμήρια.
κύκλος τις ὡς τόρνοισιν ἐκμετρούμενος,
οὗτος δ᾽ ἔχει σημεῖον ἐν μέσῳ σαφές·
τὸ δεύτερον δὲ πρῶτα μὲν γραμμαὶ δύο,
ταύτας διείργει δ᾽ ἐν μέσαις ἄλλη μία·
τρίτον δὲ βόστρυχός τις ὣς εἱλιγμένος·
τὸ δ᾽ αὖ τέταρτον ἦ μὲν εἰς ὀρθὸν μία,
λοξαὶ δ᾽ ἐπ᾽ αὐτῆς τρεῖς κατεστηριγμέναι
εἰσίν· τὸ πέμπτον δ᾽ οὐκ ἐν εὐμαρεῖ φράσαι·
γραμμαὶ γάρ εἰσιν ἐκ διεστώτων δύο,
αὗται δὲ συντρέχουσιν εἰς μίαν βάσιν·
τὸ λοίσθιον δὲ τῷ τρίτῳ προσεμφερές.

I'm not skilled at letters but I will explain the shapes
and clear symbols to you.
There is a circle marked out as it were with a compass
and it has a clear sign in the middle.
The second one is first of all two strokes
and then another one keeping them apart in the
middle.
The third is curly like a lock of hair
and the fourth is one line going straight up
and three crosswise ones attached to it.

The fifth is not easy to describe:
there are two strokes which run together from
    separate points
to one support.
And the last one is like the third.
                      (*TGF*, fr. 382)

The man has spelled out the six letters of the name 'Theseus': ΘΗΣΕΥΣ. It must have been a scene that proved dramatically effective, for two other tragedians imitated it very closely, as our extant fragments show (Agathon, *TGF* fr. 4 and Theodektes, *TGF* fr. 6; cf. Ath. 10.454b). Sophokles is said to have staged a satyr-play in which an actor danced the letters of the alphabet (*TGF*, fr. 156; Ath. 10.454f). The Athenian comic playwright Kallias produced something known as "The Alphabetic Revue" in which the twenty-four members of the chorus acted out the letters of the alphabet and imitated syllables by dancing in pairs of vowel plus consonant (Ath. 453c). Presumably, some considerable proportion of the audience at these plays could participate in the fascination and chagrin of tracing out alphabetic shapes. Perhaps they had practiced it themselves when learning letters. Perhaps they had been daunted by the task and never learned letters. Perhaps they listened to their children complaining about it at the dinner table every night. In any event, the people to whom such theater appealed were people whose imaginations could be seized by the spectacle of *grammata* taking shape in air as if they were real. These are vividly pictorial imaginations and they evidently take some pleasure in the plastic contours of the alphabet.

If we give some consideration to ancient writing as a physical production, we see this same imagination at work. The Greeks plainly regarded their alphabet as a set of pictorial devices. Through the sixth century B.C. they used for their inscriptions the continuous to-and-fro style of writing known as *boustrophēdon*, so named because it turns at the end of each line and comes back along the furrow as the ox turns with the plow (Pausanias 5.17.6). All the letters in the odd-numbered lines would face in one direction, and those in even-numbered lines in the opposite direction. Writing this way was made easier for the Greek writer by the fact that, of the twenty-six shapes available to him, twelve were symmetrical, six required very little change in reversal and only eight looked markedly different backwards. Such a style suggests a writer who thinks of his letters as a series of novel, reversible shapes: a Greek way of thinking about letters. Greek society does not seem to have borrowed this style from any other system of writing. "Its adoption," says L. H. Jeffrey, "implies simply a pictorial conception of the letters as outlined figures which can be turned in either direction according to need" (1961,46).

Attentiveness to outline in early Greek writers is apparent not only at the level of individual letters but also in the approach to groups of words and lines of text. It is a notable feature of archaic inscriptions that they frequently mark divisions between word groups with patterns of dots set one atop another in small columns of two, three, or six. This practice died out in classical times as writers and readers became blasé about their power to impose or deny edges. Some care is also given in early inscriptions to demarcating whole lines of text, and this is not merely an accident of the *boustrophēdon* style where alternate lines are distinguished by the direction of the writing. Even after this style had given way almost everywhere to a consistent left-to-right script (by the fifth century), writers continued to approximate the distinction with alternating colors of ink. Stone-cut letters, too, were at times colored with paint in alternate lines of red and black. "Some aesthetic attraction" is the motive adduced by epigraphists (e.g., Woodhead 1981, 27) for such peculiarities. But we should take note of the particular mode of the aesthetic. In writing, beauty prefers an edge.

Nor should we disregard the implements and materials of ancient writing. They wrote on stone, wood, metal, leather, ceramics, waxed tablets and papyrus. By the fifth century papyrus was the accepted medium (see Herodotos 5.58; cf. Aesch. *Supp.* 947) and the Greeks took their word for 'book' from *byblos*, 'papyrus plant.' Papyrus, both the material itself and the idea of writing on it, came originally from Gebal in Phoenicia and later from Egypt, but the Greeks did not use papyrus in the same way as the Egyptians or Phoenicians did. Instead, they rethought the activity and redesigned the materials, as they had done when they took over the Phoenician sign-system and transformed it into the world's first alphabet. A radical innovation was introduced: for use on papyrus Greek writers devised the pen (Turner 1952, 10).

The Egyptians wrote with the stem of a rush. Its ends were cut at a slant and chewed to create a fine brushlike tool. With this soft brush the Egyptian writer painted rather than wrote his letters, producing a thick and often uneven band of ink that left forked trails wherever it was lifted. Greek writers devised a pen out of the stiff, hollow reed called *kalamos* (see Pl., *Phdr.* 275). It was sharpened to a point with a knife and split at the tip. The reed-pen produced a fine line without raggedness where the pen was lifted. "But if the hand stops still for a moment, either in beginning or finishing a stroke, a little round blob of ink collects . . ." warns the papyrologist E. G. Turner (1952, 11). The reed-pen would seem to be a tool expressly designed for keeping the edges of letters cleanly demarcated. It is also a tool whose user must pay attention to exactly where he wants to stop and start each letter-stroke. Blobs of ink mar the quality of the written product as well as the enjoyment of producing it. Expertise tells, at the edge: there is the juncture of a writer's pleasure, risk and pain.

It is arguable, then, from the way they wrote and the tools they used, that ancient readers and writers conceived the Greek alphabet as a system of outlines or edges. But let us penetrate beyond the physical procedure of their writing to the activity of mind that informs it. It is an activity of symbolization. Being a phonetic system, the Greek alphabet is concerned to symbolize not objects in the real world but the very process in which sounds act to construct speech. Phonetic script imitates the activity of discourse itself. The Greek alphabet revolutionized this imitative function through introduction of its consonant, which is a theoretic element, an abstraction. The consonant functions by means of an act of imagination in the mind of the user. I am writing this book because that act astounds me. It is an act in which the mind reaches out from what is present and actual to something else. The fact that eros operates by means of an analogous act of imagination will soon be seen to be the most astounding thing about eros.

What Does the Lover
Want from Love?

My astonishing victory over Menti did not give me a
pleasure one-hundredth part as intense as the pain she
gave me when she left me for M. de Rospiec.

Stendahl, *The Life of Henri Brulard*

On the surface of it, the lover wants the beloved. This, of
course, is not really the case. If we look carefully at a
lover in the midst of desire, for example Sappho in her
fragment 31, we see how severe an experience for her is
confrontation with the beloved even at a distance. Union
would be annihilating. What the lover in this poem needs
is to be able to face the beloved and yet not be destroyed,
that is, she needs to attain the condition of "the man who
listens closely." His ideal impassivity constitutes for her
a glimpse of a new possible self. Could she realize that
self, she too would be "equal to gods" amidst desire; to
the degree that she fails to realize it, she may be destroyed
by desire. Both possibilities are projected on a screen of
what is actual and present by means of the poet's tactic
of triangulation. That godlike self, never known before,
now comes into focus and vanishes again in one quick
shift of view. As the planes of vision jump, the actual self
and the ideal self and the difference between them connect in one triangle momentarily. The connection is eros.
To feel its current pass through her is what the lover
wants.

The essential features that define this eros have already

emerged in the course of our exploration of bittersweetness. Simultaneous pleasure and pain are its symptom. Lack is its animating, fundamental constituent. As syntax, it impressed us as something of a subterfuge: properly a noun, eros acts everywhere like a verb. Its action is to reach, and the reach of desire involves every lover in an activity of the imagination.

It is no new idea that the imagination has a powerful role to play in human desire. Homer's description of Helen in the *Iliad* is perhaps the archetypal demonstration of it. The description is withheld. Homer merely tells us that the old men on the wall of Troy watched her pass and let out a whisper:

οὐ νέμεσις Τρῶας καὶ ἐϋκνήμιδας Ἀχαιοὺς
τοιῆδ᾽ ἀμφὶ γυναικὶ πολὺν χρόνον ἄλγεα πάσχειν·

It is no discredit for Trojans and well-greaved Achaeans
to suffer long anguish for a woman like that.
(*Il.* 3.156-57)

Helen remains universally desired, universally imaginable, perfect.

Erotic theorists spend considerable time discovering and rediscovering the lover's imagination from different angles. Aristotle defines the dynamic and imaginative delight of desire in his *Rhetoric*. "Desire is a reaching out [*orexis*] for the sweet," he says, and the man who is reaching for some delight, whether in the future as hope or in the past as memory, does so by means of an act of imagination (*phantasia: Rh.* 1.1370a6). Andreas Capellanus analyzes the pain of amorous longing in the same light in his twelfth-century treatise *De Amore*, insisting that this *passio* is a thoroughly mental event: "The suffering of love does not arise out of any action . . . but only from the cogitation of the mind upon what it sees does that suffering issue." (XIV). Stendhal, in his celebrated essay on love, uncovers in the lover a fantasizing process that he names "crystallization" after a phenomenon witnessed in the mines of Salzburg:

> Leave a lover with his thoughts for twenty-four hours and this is what will happen: At the salt mines of Salzburg, they throw a leafless wintry bough into one of the abandoned workings. Two or three months later they pull it out covered with a shining deposit of crystals. The smallest twig, no bigger than a tom-tit's claw, is studded with a galaxy of scintillating diamonds. The original branch is no longer recognizable. What I have called crystallization is a mental process which draws from everything that happens new proofs of the perfection of the loved one. (1957, 45)

Kierkegaard also devotes some thought to this "sensuously idealizing power . . . [that] beautifies and develops the one desired so that he flushes in enhanced beauty by its reflection." The force by which Don Juan seduces may be found in this "energy of sensuous desire," Kierkegaard concludes, with a trace of relief (1944, 86-102). Freudian theory, too, takes note of this projective faculty of the human erotic instinct, ascribing to it the scheduled mischief known as 'transference' in psychoanalytic situations. Transference arises in almost every psychoanalytic relationship when the patient insists on falling in love with the doctor, despite the latter's determined aloofness, warnings and discouragement. An important lesson in erotic mistrust is available to the analysand who observes himself concocting in this way a love object out of thin air.

Such concoctions fascinate the modern novelist. Anna Karenina's passion for Vronsky depends on a mental act:

> She put her hands on his shoulders and looked at him for a long time with a profound, passionate and

at the same time searching look. She was studying his face to make up for the time she hadn't seen him. She was doing what she always did when she saw him—comparing the image of him in her imagination (incomparably superior, and impossible in reality) with him as he was. (pt. 4, chap. 2)

Emma Bovary's love letters to Rodolphe enact the same process: "But as she wrote she saw in her mind's eye another man, a phantom composed of her most passionate memories, her most enjoyable books, and her strongest desires; at last he became so real and so tangible that she was thrilled and amazed, yet he was so hidden under the abundance of his virtues that she was unable to imagine him clearly" (quoted in Girard 1965, 63-64). The heroine of Italo Calvino's novel *The Nonexistent Knight* is a splendid voluptuary who finds she can only feel genuine desire for the knight of the title, an empty suit of armour; all others are either known or knowable and cannot arouse her. Here we arrive at the nub of the matter, not for the first time. That which is known, attained, possessed, cannot be an object of desire. "In love possession is nothing, only delight matters," says Stendhal (1957, 112). Eros is lack, says Sokrates. This dilemma is given a still more subtle image by Yasunari Kawabata. His novel *Beauty and Sadness* (1975) recounts the early days of the marriage of Oki and Fumiko. Oki is a novelist and Fumiko a typist in a news agency. She types all his manuscripts and this connection is the substance of Oki's newlywed fascination with his bride:

> It was something of a lover's game, the sweet togetherness of newlyweds, but there was more to it than that. When his work first appeared in a magazine he was astonished at the difference in effect between a penwritten manuscript and the tiny characters in print. (34)

As Oki becomes habituated to this "gap between manuscript and published work" his passion for Fumiko fades and he takes a mistress.

It is in the difference between cursive and typeface, between the real Vronsky and the imaginary one, between Sappho and "the man who listens closely," between an actual knight and an empty suit of armour, that desire is felt. Across this space a spark of eros moves in the lover's mind to activate delight. Delight is a movement (*kinēsis*) of the soul, in Aristotle's definition (*Rh.* 1.1369b19). No difference: no movement. No Eros.

A mood of knowledge is emitted by the spark that leaps in the lover's soul. He feels on the verge of grasping something not grasped before. In the Greek poets it is a knowledge of self that begins to come into focus, a self not known before and now disclosed by the lack of it— by pain, by a hole, bitterly. Not all lovers respond to erotic knowledge so negatively. We were struck by the equanimity with which Virginia Woolf's character, Neville, records "Something now leaves me" (1931, 83) and we saw what a gust of elation accompanies the change of self for Nietzsche (1967, 426). But then, Nietzsche calls the modern world an ass that says yes to everyhing. The Greek poets do not say yes. They allow that erotic experience is sweet to begin with: *gluku.* They acknowledge ideal possibilities opened out for selfhood by erotic experience; they do so, in general, by divinizing it in the person of the god Eros. Sappho, as we have seen, projects the ideal in the particular person of "the man who listens closely" in fragment 31. A more narcissistic lover, namely Alkibiades in Plato's *Symposium*, subsumes the ideal to himself, blandly announcing his motive for pursuing Sokrates:

ἐμοὶ μὲν γὰρ οὐδέν ἐστι πρεσβύτερον τοῦ ὡς ὅτι βέλτιστον ἐμὲ γενέσθαι

For me nothing has a higher priority than to perfect myself. (*Symp.* 218d)

But a sense of exultation at the thought of incorporating the self's possibilities within the self's identity is missing. In these ancient representations, bittersweet Eros prints consistently as a negative image. Presumably, a positive picture could be made if the lover were ever to reincorporate his lack into a new and better self. Or could it? Is that positive picture what the lover wants from love? An ancient answer presents itself. Aristophanes puts this very question to a pair of imaginary lovers in Plato's *Symposium*. He pictures the lovers locked in an embrace and dismisses as absurd the notion that this "mere amorous union" (*sunousia tōn aphrodisiōn*, 192c) is all they want:

ἀλλ᾿ ἄλλο τι βουλομένη ἑκατέρου ἡ ψυχὴ δήλη ἐστίν, ὃ οὐ δύναται εἰπεῖν, ἀλλὰ μαντεύεται ὃ βούλεται, καὶ αἰνίττεται.

No, obviously the soul of each is longing for something else which it cannot put into normal words but keeps trying to express in oracles and riddles.

(192c-d)

What is this "something else"? Aristophanes continues:

καὶ εἰ αὐτοῖς ἐν τῷ αὐτῷ κατακειμένοις ἐπιστὰς ὁ Ἥφαιστος, ἔχων τὰ ὄργανα, ἔροιτο· "Τί ἔσθ᾿ ὃ βούλεσθε, ὦ ἄνθρωποι, ὑμῖν παρ᾿ ἀλλήλων γενέσθαι;" καὶ εἰ ἀποροῦντας αὐτοὺς πάλιν ἔροιτο· "Ἆρά γε τοῦδε ἐπιθυμεῖτε, ἐν τῷ αὐτῷ γενέσθαι ὅτι μάλιστα ἀλλήλοις, ὥστε καὶ νύκτα καὶ ἡμέραν μὴ ἀπολείπεσθαι ἀλλήλων; εἰ γὰρ τούτου ἐπιθυμεῖτε, θέλω ὑμᾶς συντῆξαι καὶ συμφῦσαι εἰς τὸ αὐτό, ὥστε δύ᾿ ὄντας ἕνα γεγονέναι καὶ ἕως τ᾿ ἂν ζῆτε, ὡς ἕνα ὄντα, κοινῇ ἀμφοτέρους ζῆν, καὶ ἐπειδὰν ἀποθάνητε, ἐκεῖ

αὖ ἐν Ἅιδου ἀντὶ δυοῖν ἕνα εἶναι κοινῇ τεθνεῶτε·
ἀλλ᾿ ὁρᾶτε εἰ τούτου ἐρᾶτε καὶ ἐξαρκεῖ ὑμῖν ἂν
τούτου τύχητε·"

Suppose that, as the lovers lay together, Hephaistos
should come and stand over them, tools in hand,
and ask: "O human beings, what is it you want of
one another?" And suppose they were nonplussed,
so he put the question again: "Well, is this what you
crave, to be joined in the closest possible union with
one another, so as not to leave one another by night
or day? If that is your craving, I am ready to melt
you together and fuse you into a single unit, so that
two become one and as long as you live you may
both, as one, live a common life, and when you die
you may also, down there in Hades, one instead of
two, die a common death. Consider whether this is
what you desire, whether it would satisfy you to ob-
tain this." (192d-e)

Eternal oneness is Hephaistos' offer. The lovers' response is not heard. Instead, Aristophanes himself inter-
venes to pronounce: "No lover could want anything
else" (192e). Now, how credible a witness is Aristophanes, or his spokesman Hephaistos, in the question of
what a lover really wants? Two reservations strike us:
Hephaistos, impotent cuckold of the Olympian pan-
theon, can be viewed as at best a qualified authority on
matters erotic; and Aristophanes' judgment ("no lover
could want anything else") is belied by the anthropology
of his own myth. Was it the case that the round beings of
his fantasy remained perfectly content rolling about the
world in prelapsarian oneness? No. They got big ideas
and started rolling toward Olympus to make an attempt
on the gods (190b-c). They began reaching for something
else. So much for oneness.

Paraphrase?

It is not the number 'one,' as we have seen in example

after example, to which the lover's mind inclines when he is given a chance to express his desire. Maneuvers of triangulation disclose him. For his delight is in reaching; to reach for something perfect would be perfect delight. The sweet apple still dangling in Sappho's fragment 105a represents this wrenching, delightful fact. We have looked at some of the tactics of incompleteness by which Sappho sustains desire and desirability in the poem. We have looked at similar tactics penetrating lovers' logic and contracting upon a solitude unknown before. They are tactics of imagination, which sometimes turn upon enhancing the beloved, sometimes upon reconceiving the lover, but which are all aimed at defining one certain edge or difference: an edge between two images that cannot merge in a single focus because they do not derive from the same level of reality—one is actual, one is possible. To know both, keeping the difference visible, is the subterfuge called eros.

Symbolon

Space reaches out from us and translates the world.

Rilke, "What Birds Plunge Through
Is Not the Intimate Space"

We began our investigation of bittersweet Eros by coun-
tenancing a mistranslation of Sappho's *glukupikron*. We
assumed that Sappho puts *gluku-* first because Eros'
sweetness is obvious to everyone, his bitterness less so.
We then turned our attention to the bitter side. These
judgments were shallow, as we are now in a position to
see. Eros' sweetness is inseparable from his bitterness,
and each participates, in a way not yet obvious at all, in
our human will to knowledge. There would seem to be
some resemblance between the way Eros acts in the mind
of a lover and the way knowing acts in the mind of a
thinker. It has been an endeavour of philosophy from the
time of Sokrates to understand the nature and uses of
that resemblance. But not only philosophers are in-
trigued to do so. I would like to grasp why it is that these
two activities, falling in love and coming to know, make
me feel genuinely alive. There is something like an electrification in them. They are not like anything else, but
they are like each other. How? Let us consider whether
the ancient poets' conception of *glukupikrotēs*, as we
have come to understand it, has any light to shed on this
matter.

"All men by their very nature reach out to know," says
Aristotle (*Metaph. A* 1.980a21). If this is so, it discloses
something important about the activities of knowing and

desiring. They have at their core the same delight, that of
reaching, and entail the same pain, that of falling short
or being deficient. This disclosure may be already im-
plied in a certain usage of Homer, for epic diction has the
same verb (*mnaomai*) for 'to be mindful, to have in mind,
to direct one's attention to' and 'to woo, court, be a
suitor.' Stationed at the edge of itself, or of its present
knowledge, the thinking mind launches a suit for understanding into the unknown. So too the wooer stands at
the edge of his value as a person and asserts a claim
across the boundaries of another. Both mind and wooer
reach out from what is known and actual to something
different, possibly better, desired. Something else. Think
about what that feels like.

When we try to think about our own thinking, as
when we try to feel our own desire, we find ourselves located at a blind point. It is like the point where the observer of Velazquez' painting *Las Meninas* stands as he
views the painting. This is a painting of Velazquez painting the king and queen of Spain. But the king and queen
are not part of the picture. Or are they? There are many
people, including Velazquez, in the painting but none
seem to be the king and queen, and all are gazing steadily
out at someone else beyond the picture frame. Who? As
we meet the looks of these people we imagine at first that
they are gazing at us. Then we notice some faces in a mirror at the back of the room. Whose are the faces? Our
own? No. These are the king and queen of Spain. But
now, just where are the king and queen located? They
seem to be standing precisely where we are standing as
we gaze into the painting at their reflection there. Then
where are we? For that matter, who are we?

We are no one in particular and we are standing at a
blind point. Michel Foucault has analyzed Velazquez'
painting and its blind point in his study of the archaeology of human knowledge, *The Order of Things*. Foucault calls the blind point "that essential hiding place

into which our gaze disappears from ourselves at the moment of actual looking" (4). We cannot see that point, as we cannot think thought or desire desire, except by a subterfuge. In *Las Meninas* we see the subterfuge just coming into focus in a mirror at the back of the room. In Foucault's terms this mirror provides "a metathesis of visibility" because around it the painting organizes a deliberate vacancy: "The lines that run through the depth of the picture are not complete; they all lack a segment of their trajectories. This gap is caused by the absence of the king—an absence that is an artifice on the part of the painter" (16).

Velazquez' artifice triangulates our perception so that we all but see ourselves looking. That is, he has arranged his painting in such a way that a haunting fact gradually dawns on us as we observe it. Namely the fact that the vacancy recorded by the mirror is not that of King Philip IV and Queen Mariana. It is our own. Standing like understudies in the place where the king and queen would be, we recognize (vaguely disappointed) that the faces looming from the mirror are not our own and we all but see (if the angle did not keep jumping out of focus) that point where we disappear into ourselves in order to look. A point lying in the gap between ourselves and them. Attempts to focus on that point pull the mind into vertigo, while at the same time a particular acute delight is present. We long to see that point, although it tears us. Why?

There is no stillness at that point. Its components split and diverge each time we try to bring them into focus, as if interior continents were wrenching askew in the mind. It is not a point upon which we can gaze in such a way as to peacefully converge with the king and queen in one image there, one noun. That point is a verb. Each time we look at it, it acts. How?

Let us keep these questions in mind as we consider another point on the landscape of human thinking, a point which is also a verb—moreover a verb that triangulates,

haunts, splits, wrenches and delights us each time it acts.
Let us consider the point of verbal action called 'metaphor.'

"To give names to nameless things by transference
[*metaphora*] from things kindred or similar in appearance" is how Aristotle describes the function of metaphor (*Rh.* 3.2.1405a34). In current theory, this process
of thought may best be regarded as an interaction between the subject and the predicate of the metaphorical
sentence. Metaphorical sense is produced by the whole
sentence and works through what one critic calls a "semantic impertinence" (Cohen 1966), that is, a violation
of the code of pertinence or relevance that rules the ascription of predicates in ordinary use in the language.
The violation allows a new pertinence or congruence to
emerge, which is the metaphorical meaning, from the
collapse of the ordinary or literal meaning. How does the
new pertinence emerge? There is in the mind a change or
shift of distance, which Aristotle calls an *epiphora* (*Poet.*
21.1457b7), bringing two heterogeneous things close to
reveal their kinship. The innovation of metaphor occurs
in this shift of distance from far to near, and it is effected
by imagination. A virtuoso act of imagination brings the
two things together, sees their incongruence, then sees
also a new congruence, meanwhile continuing to recognize the previous incongruence through the new congruence. Both the ordinary, literal sense and a novel sense
are present at once in the words of a metaphor; both the
ordinary, descriptive reference and a novel reference are
held in tension by the metaphor's way of looking at the
world.

Thus, tension of an acute and unresolvable kind informs this mental action. It demands of the mind a "stereoscopic vision" (as Stanford 1936 puts it) or a "split reference" (in Jakobsen's terms), that is, an ability to hold
in equipoise two perspectives at once. Paul Ricoeur calls
this condition of mental tension a state of war wherein

the mind has not yet reached conceptual peace but is caught between distance and proximity, between sameness and difference. Such warfare marks the landscape of all human thought, according to Ricoeur:

> We may speak with Gadamer of the fundamental metaphoricity of thought to the extent that the figure of speech that we call 'metaphor' allows us a glance at the general procedure by which we produce concepts. This is because in the metaphoric process the movement toward genus is arrested by the resistance of the difference and, as it were, intercepted by the figure of rhetoric. (Ricoeur 1978, 149)

An act of arrest and interception that splits the mind and puts it in a state of war within itself is the act called 'metaphor.' Let us compare with this act our experience of *Las Meninas*. At the core of the act called 'metaphor' our minds reach toward an identification: "to give names to nameless things" as Aristotle says. Velazquez' artifice, in its turn, provokes us to try to give a name to that object at which all the eyes looking out of the painting are looking. For a moment we imagine they are all looking at us. Then we see the faces in the mirror. Our movement toward naming those faces is arrested by the difference between the two species (ourselves, the king and queen) who are candidates for that genus. The arrest occurs with a wrench that splits our vision, divides our judgment and is not resolved no matter how often we return to it for, each time we look, our moment of delighted self-recognition is intercepted by two dimly royal faces in the glass. Aristotle pinpoints such a moment of interception in metaphorical thinking, when the mind seems to say to itself: "Well how true! I was quite wrong after all!" He calls it a paradoxical element (*ti paradoxon*) and judges it one of the essential pleasures of metaphor (*Rh.* 3.2.1412a6).

Symbolon

Eros also has "something paradoxical" at the core of his power, at that point where bitter intercepts sweet. There is a shift of distance that brings up close what is absent and different. "Absences of eyes in the statues" present Helen to Menelaos as he stands in his empty hall, at the blind point between love and hate (Aesch. *Ag.* 414-19). "They love him and they hate him and they long to possess him" says Aristophanes of the love affair between the Greek *dēmos* and its favorite Alkibiades (*Ran.* 1425). "I'm in love, I'm not in love! I'm insane, I'm not insane!" cries out Anakreon (413 *PMG*). Something paradoxical arrests the lover. Arrest occurs at a point of inconcinnity between the actual and the possible, a blind point where the reality of what we are disappears into the possibility of what we could be if we were other than we are. But we are not. We are not the king and queen of Spain. We are not lovers who can both feel and attain their desires. We are not poets who need no metaphor or symbol to carry our meaning across.

The English word 'symbol' is the Greek word *symbolon* which means, in the ancient world, one half of a knucklebone carried as a token of identity to someone who has the other half. Together the two halves compose one meaning. A metaphor is a species of symbol. So is a lover. In the words of Aristophanes (in Plato's *Symposium*):

ἕκαστος οὖν ἡμῶν ἐστιν ἀνθρώπου σύμβολον, ἅτε τετμημένος ὥσπερ αἱ ψῆτται, ἐξ ἑνὸς δύο· ζητεῖ δὴ ἀεὶ τὸ αὑτοῦ ἕκαστος σύμβολον.

Each one of us is but the *symbolon* of a human being—sliced in half like a flatfish, two instead of one—and each pursues a neverending search for the *symbolon* of himself.   (191d)

Every hunting, hungering lover is half of a knucklebone, wooer of a meaning that is inseparable from its absence. The moment when we understand these things—when we see what we are projected on a screen of what we could be—is invariably a moment of wrench and arrest. We love that moment, and we hate it. We have to keep going back to it, after all, if we wish to maintain contact with the possible. But this also entails watching it disappear. Only a god's word has no beginning or end. Only a god's desire can reach without lack. Only the paradoxical god of desire, exception to all these rules, is neverendingly filled with lack itself.

"Sappho drew this conception together and called Eros *glukupikron*."[8]

[8] So says Maximus of Tyre, a Sophist and itinerant lecturer of the second century A.D. (18.9; Sappho *LP*, fr. 172).

A Novel Sense

Nature has no outline, but Imagination has.

William Blake, *Notebooks*

Imagination is the core of desire. It acts at the core of metaphor. It is essential to the activity of reading and writing. In the archaic lyric poetry of Greece, these three trajectories intersected, perhaps fortuitously, and imagination transcribed on human desire an outline more beautiful (some people think) than any before or since. We have seen what shape that outline took. Writing about desire, the archaic poets made triangles with their words. Or, to put it less sharply, they represent situations that ought to involve two factors (lover, beloved) in terms of three (lover, beloved and the space between them, however realized). Is this outline just a fetish of the lyric imagination? No. We have looked at tragedians and comic poets and epigrammatists concerned with the bittersweetness of desire. We have discovered the roots of the notion in Homer's Aphrodite. We have seen Plato turn the problem over. There is something essential to eros here.

The lyric poets caught its outline with sudden sharpness, and left that in writing. 'What does the lover want from love?' is the question to which the lyric evidence led us. But now we should consider the matter from another side, for the nature of the lyric evidence cannot be separated from the fact of its transcription, and that fact remains mysterious. I mean by this that the lyric poets present a borderline case, living as they did in the first outburst of literary activity that followed the alphabet, commissioned as they were to compose lyrics for oral and public performance but somehow involved also in making written record of these poems. They are poets exploring the edge between oral and literate procedure, probing forward to see what kind of thing writing is, reading is, poetry can be. The position is not an easy one. Perhaps that is why the poems are so good. At any rate, the position gradually became easier as literacy spread throughout the Greek world. New genres of expression developed to meet its demands. Let us look at the most influential of those genres, evolved expressly for the delectation of writers and readers. Let us superimpose on the question 'What does the lover want from love' the questions 'What does the reader want from reading? What is the writer's desire?' Novels are the answer.

"I composed it in writing [*synegrapsa*]," says the Greek author Chariton at the beginning of his *Chaereas and Callirhoe*, earliest extant example of the genre that we call the novel or romance. The novel was from the beginning a written literature, which flourished in the Graeco-Roman world from about the third century B.C., when the spread of literacy and a vigorous book trade created a wide popular audience. Our terms 'novel' and 'romance' do not reflect an ancient name for the genre. Chariton refers to his work as *erōtika pathēmata*, or "erotic sufferings": these are love stories in which it is generically required that love be painful. The stories are told in prose and their apparent aim is to entertain readers.

Four Greek novels from the ancient world are extant, as well as some fragments and epitomes dating from about the first century B.C. to the fourth century A.D., and a number of Latin romances. The plots are much the same, being love stories devoted to keeping the lovers apart and miserable until the last page. One editor has summed up the genre this way:

A romantic love story is the thread on which is hung a succession of sentimental and sensational episodes; the two main characters either fall in love with one another soon after the opening of the story, or in some cases are actually married and immediately separated; they are sundered time and again by the most improbable misfortunes; they face death in every form; subsidiary couples are sometimes introduced, the course of whose true love runs very little smoother; both the hero and heroine inspire a wicked and hopeless love in the breasts of others, who become hostile influences, seeming at times likely to accomplish their final separation, but never with complete success; occasionally the narrative stops for the description of a place, a scene, or some natural object only to be resumed at once with the painful adventures of the loving couple; and on the last page all is cleared up, the complicated threads of the story fall apart with detailed and lengthy explanations, and the happy pair is united for ever with the prospect of a long and prosperous life before them. (Gaselee 1917, 411)

Tactics of triangulation are the main business of the novel. These tactics are the ones familiar to us from the archaic poets, now employed prosaically and *in extenso*. The novelists play out as dilemmas of plot and character all those facets of erotic contradiction and difficulty that were first brought to light in lyric poetry. Rival lovers appear around every corner of the plot. Pretexts for pursuit and flight ramify from page to page. Obstacles to romantic union materialize in tireless variety. The lovers themselves devote considerable energy to obstructing their own desire—should interfering parents, cruel pirates, bungling doctors, dogged graverobbers, dull slaves, mindless divinities and the whims of chance not suffice. *Aidōs* is a favorite stratagem. Romantic heroes and her-

A Novel Sense

oines operate in a vague, exciting borderland between purity and sensuality. Whenever passion seems within reach, *aidōs* falls like a veil between them. This *aidōs* is the archaic ethic of 'shamefastness' reinterpreted now in the narrow sense of chastity. Its mischievous machinery pervades romantic plots and exacts feats of virtue from lovers in return for protraction of the story.

"Aphrodisian chastity" is the name given by one critic to this pleasing torment, for Aphrodite is the divinity in charge of the perversities of *aidōs* within the novel. She is chief designer and chief subverter of the story's changing triangles, both patron and enemy, inspiring lovers with a passion strong enough to resist all the temptations that she herself proceeds to hurl against it. Chaste lovers make her the object of their devotion, and become the object of her abuse.

Aphrodite's role in novels is an ambivalent, not to say paradoxical, one like the role of Eros in archaic poetry. In his *Ephesiaca*, Xenophon of Ephesus gives us a summary image of Aphrodisian ambivalence. Describing the bridal chamber of his hero and heroine, Xenophon goes into details of the *eikōn* embroidered on the bedcover. Its subject is Aphrodite, the divinity responsible for bringing bride and groom together in the chamber. But the scenario worked on the coverlet is not one that bodes well for the marriage. Aphrodite is pictured not as the dutiful wife of Hephaistos but rather as mistress of Ares. Ares is decked out for an assignation with his beloved and Eros is leading him by the hand toward her, holding up a flaming torch (1.8). Xenophon's description of the *eikōn* would strike a note of recognition in any Greek reader. It evokes a scene pictured on numbers of ancient vases and no doubt familiar from daily life: the scene of the wedding procession, wherein a new bride was led by the hand to her husband's house, preceded by flaming torches. The *eikōn* is a parody of standard wedding ritual, in concept and in design. So much for marriage.

Yet marriage remains the professed objective of every romantic hero and heroine. This puts them at odds with themselves and with Aphrodite. More important, the intention to consummate desire puts the lovers at odds with the novelist, whose novel will end unless he can subvert their aim. There is something paradoxical in the relations between a novelist and his lovers. As a writer he knows their story must end and wants it to end. So, too, as readers we know the novel must end and want it to end. "But not yet!" say the readers to the writer. "But not yet!" says the writer to his hero and heroine. "But not yet!" says the beloved to the lover. And so the reach of desire continues. What is a paradox? A paradox is a kind of thinking that reaches out but never arrives at the end of its thought. Each time it reaches out, there is a shift of distance in mid-reasoning that prevents the answer from being grasped. Consider Zeno's well-known paradoxes. They are arguments against the reality of reaching an end. Zeno's runner never gets to the finish line of the stadium, Zeno's Achilles never overtakes the tortoise, Zeno's arrow never hits the target (see Arist., *Ph.* 239b5-18; 263a4-6). These are paradoxes about paradox. Each one contains a point where the reasoning seems to fold into itself and disappear, or at least that is how it feels. Each time it disappears, it can begin again, and so the reach continues. If you happen to enjoy reasoning, you are delighted to begin again. On the other hand, your enjoyment of reasoning must entail some wish to arrive at a conclusion, so your delight has an edge of chagrin.

In the bittersweetness of the exercise we see the outline of eros. You love Zeno and you hate him. You know there is a ruse operating in his paradoxes, yet you keep going back over them. And you keep going back to the paradoxes not because you would like to see Achilles overtake the tortoise but because you like trying to understand what kind of thing a paradox is.

You like being situated at that blind but lively point

where your reason is viewing itself—or almost viewing itself. Why? We have come round to this blind point before, when contemplating Velazquez' *Las Meninas* and considering the paradoxical action at the heart of metaphor. Novels give us another, and broader, access onto the blind point, for they sustain the experience of paradox over many pages, by means of many ruses. Let us see what we can read from the ruses of the novelists about the blind point and its desirability.

Something Paradoxical

Critics of the novel find paradox to be "a principle of the genre" and note the frequency with which the romances speak of situations as "new and strange" (*kainos*) or "against reason" (*paralogos*), or "unthought of" (*adoketos*) (Heiserman 1977, 77 and 226 n. 4). Techniques of paradox enrich these stories at all levels of plot, imagery and wordplay. Paradox is especially essential to their emotional texture. This can surprise no one familiar with the lyric precedents of erotic fiction. "I'm crazy! I'm not crazy! I'm in love! I'm not in love!" said Anakreon in the sixth century B.C. (413 *PMG*). "I don't know what I should do. Two states of mind in me . . ." said Sappho (*LP*, fr. 51). Characters in novels luxuriate in such moments of emotional schizophrenia, when the personality is split into two warring factions. Novelists expand these moments into full-scale soliloquies of the soul, so that a character may debate his erotic dilemma with himself, usually at length and to no purpose. But emotional schism is not the exclusive property of heroes and heroines in novels. All who observe their fortunes, within and without the text, are programmed to respond in this way.

Take, for example, the ending of Xenophon's *Ephesiaca*. As the heroine Anthia falls into her lover's arms, the townspeople standing around are stirred by "pleasure, pain, fear, memory of the past, apprehension of the future, all mixing in their souls" (5.13). So too at the end of Heliodoros' *Aethiopica*, the lovers' union is witnessed by their fellow citizens, in whom:

... ὑφ᾽ ἧς καὶ τὰ ἐναντιώτατα πρὸς συμφωνίαν
ἡρμόζετο, χαρᾶς καὶ λύπης συμπεπλεγμένων, γέλωτι
δακρύων κεραννυμένων, τῶν στυγνοτάτων εἰς ἑορ-
τὴν μεταβαλλομένων

... absolute contrarieties were fitted together as one
sound: joy interwoven with grief, tears mixed with
laughter, total gloom turning into festive delight.
... (10.38.4)

Earlier in Heliodoros' novel a certain character named
Calasiris records his reaction to the erotic sufferings of
the heroine:

... ἡδονῆς δὲ ἅμα καὶ λύπης ἐνεπλήσθην. καὶ πάθος
τι καινότερον ὑπέστην, ὁμοῦ δακρύων καὶ χαίρων

... at the same time I was filled with pleasure and
pain: I found myself in quite a novel state of mind
[pathos ti kainoteron] weeping and rejoicing simultaneously.... (4.9.1)

As readers we too are meant to feel this paradoxical
mix of feelings, if the novelist is in proper command of
his ruses. So Chariton implies when he turns to us, at a
particularly brilliant moment in the action of his plot,
and demands:

Ποῖος ποιητὴς ἐπὶ σκηνῆς παράδοξον μῦθον οὕτως
εἰσήγαγεν; ἔδοξας ἂν ἐν θεάτρῳ παρεῖναι μυρίων
παλῶν πλήρει. πάντα ἦν ὁμοῦ· δάκρυα, χαρά,
θάμβος, ἔλεος, ἀπιστία, εὐχαί.

What poet ever produced such a paradoxical scenario [paradoxon mython] on the stage? You must
have thought you were sitting in the theater filled
with a thousand emotions, all at the same time:
tears, joy, amazement, pity, disbelief, fervent pray-
ers! (Chaereas and Callirhoe 5.8.2)

To create pleasure and pain at once is the novelist's
aim. We should dwell on this point for a moment. It is of

some importance that, as readers, we are typically and repeatedly drawn into a conflicted emotional response which approximates that of the lover's soul divided by desire. Readership itself affords the aesthetic distance and obliquity necessary for this response. The reader's emotions begin from a privileged position of knowledge. We know the story will end happily. The characters within the story do not seem to know this. So we stand at an angle to the text from which we can see both the narrated facts of the case and also what the characters believe to be the facts of the case: two levels of narrative reality float one upon another, without converging, and provide for the reader that moment of emotional and cognitive stereoscopy which is also the experience of the desiring lover.

We saw Sappho construct this stereoscopic moment in fr. 31 as a three-point circuit of desire joining herself, her beloved and "the man who listens closely." The verbal action of eros in fr. 31 allows our perception to jump or shift from one level of desire to another, from actual to possible, without losing sight of the difference between them. In Sappho's poem the shift of view is momentary, a vertigo and sudden sense of being very close to the core where feelings form. In the novel this technique of shifting distance is taken over as the permanent attitude from which the reader views the action. Novels institutionalize the ruse of eros. It becomes a narrative texture of sustained incongruence, emotional and cognitive. It permits the reader to stand in triangular relation to the characters in the story and reach into the text after the objects of their desire, sharing their longing but also detached from it, seeing their view of reality but also its mistakenness. It is almost like being in love.

My Page Makes Love

A few examples are in order. The novelist Longus (second-third century A.D.) prefaces his novel *Daphnis and Chloe* with a bold statement of the triangular tension that is its structure and raison d'être. He was moved to write the tale, he tells us, because he encountered "a painted image of the history of Eros" that struck him as the most beautiful thing he had ever seen. Longing (*pothos*) seized him to "create a rival image in writing" and he set to work on the novel. There are three components in Longus' opening conceit. There is the painted icon of Eros, an object of ideal beauty (*kalliston*) transcending all the actual beauty of woods and waters around it, Longus says. There is the verbal icon, the novel itself, reaching out to rival or to approximate the perfect beauty of the painting in an act of writing. In between the ideal and the rival icon is the motive force of desire (*pothos*) that impels Longus to try to bring these two heterogeneous images together on the screen of imagination.

The two icons are like the two parts of a metaphor: an already existing image or sense and a novel image or sense are brought close by an act of imagination. Together they compose one meaning. Longus' imaginative effort, like the verbal innovation that we call metaphor, is an erotic action, reaching out from what is known and present to something else, something different, something desired. The meaning he composes is a dynamic meaning, not a still point, that comes alive as the novel shifts from plane to plane of its various triangles. Something paradoxical is inherent in these shifts, and as readers, we are invited into its experience, standing on the edge of other people's desire, arrested, wooed, triangulated and changed by a series of marks on a piece of paper. "My Page makes love, and understands it feelingly," says Montaigne (1603, bk. 5, ch. 3). Longus' page makes love to the reader, first and obviously, by drawing him into the bittersweet emotion of lovers in the story. But this narrative voyeurism is only the surface. A much more arresting act of love is going on at depth, in the whole metaphorical undertaking of setting one icon against another. *Daphnis and Chloe* is the story of a boy and girl discovering eros. Everything they do and say sounds symbolic. All lovers believe they are inventing love: Daphnis and Chloe actually *do* invent love. They live in a pastoral wonderland, swell to desire with the buds of spring and, after many discouragements, marry one another on the last pages in a cave of Eros. They are, as one critic puts it, "emblematic innocents in emblematic predicaments undergoing an emblematic growth in erotic knowledge" (Heiserman 1977, 143). Here, for example, is what happens when Daphnis wins his father's consent to marry Chloe and rushes out to tell her the news. The lovers find themselves in an orchard rich with fruit trees:

μία μηλέα τετρύγητο καὶ οὔτε καρπὸν εἶχεν οὔτε φύλλον· γυμνοὶ πάντες ἦσαν οἱ κλάδοι. καὶ ἓν μῆλον ἐπέτετο ἐν αὐτοῖς ἄκροις ἀκρότατον, μέγα καὶ καλὸν καὶ τῶν πολλῶν τὴν εὐωδίαν ἐνίκα μόνον. ἔδεισεν ὁ τρυγῶν ἀνελθεῖν, ἠμέλησε καθελεῖν· τάχα δὲ καὶ ἐφυλάττετο ⟨τὸ⟩ καλὸν μῆλον ἐρωτικῷ ποιμένι.

There stood one apple tree whose apples had all been gathered. It had neither fruit nor leaf. All the boughs were bare. And a single apple floated on the very top of the topmost boughs: big and beautiful and more fragrant in itself than many others. The applepicker was afraid to go up so high, or he over-looked it. And perhaps that beautiful apple was sav-ing itself for a shepherd in love.

Daphnis is eager to pick the apple. Chloe forbids him. Daphnis picks the apple. To mollify Chloe he then says:

"'Ὦ παρθένε, τοῦτο τὸ μῆλον ἔφυσαν Ὧραι καλαὶ καὶ φυτὸν καλὸν ἔθρεψε πεπαίνοντος ἡλίου καὶ ἐτήρησε Τύχη. καὶ οὐκ ἔμελλον αὐτὸ καταλιπεῖν ὀφθαλμοὺς ἔχων, ἵνα πέσῃ χαμαὶ καὶ ἢ ποίμνιον αὐτὸ πατήσῃ νεμόμενον ἢ ἑρπετὸν φαρμάξῃ συρόμε-νον ἢ χρόνος δαπανήσῃ κείμενον, ὁλεπόμενον, ἐπαι-νούμενον. τοῦτο Ἀφροδίτη κάλλους ἔλαβεν ἆθλον, τοῦτο ἐγὼ σοὶ δίδωμι νικητήριον."

"O maiden, beautiful seasons begot this apple, a beautiful tree nourished it in the ripening sun and fortune kept close watch. Having eyes, I could not let it be—it might have fallen to the ground and been trampled by grazing flocks or poisoned by some creeping creature or used up by Time as it waited there, gazed at, object of praise. This was the prize Aphrodite won for beauty, this I give to you as vic-tory-prize." (3.33-34)

Daphnis drops the apple in Chloe's lap, she kisses him "and so Daphnis repented not at all of having dared to go up so high."

Daphnis is a lover who takes literary motifs literally. Here he woos his beloved with the very symbol of wooing and acts out the paradigmatic reach of desire. Longus expects you to recognize the high apple on the highest branch from Sappho's poem (fr. 105a) and to read Daphnis' action as emblematic. At the same time the apple is typical of all love gifts, well-known throughout Greek poetry and visual art as the favorite offering of lover to beloved. The apple's traditional association with Aphrodite and the judgment of Paris is another strand of erotic symbolization, evoked here by Daphnis himself. And the apple might be thought to represent Chloe as bride, blooming in the wild and soon to be plucked for marriage. The respective attitudes of lover and beloved are stereotypical too: irrepressible desire meets adamant resistance. He insists, she submits, the apple is the loser. These various levels of inference float upon the essential narrative fact: it is a real apple and wins a real kiss, or so we read.

Longus' novel is a continuous fabric of such levels, held in rich and transparent suspension against the facts of the plot, like the apple as it "floats" upon the tree. Look closer, for a moment, at this apple in Longus' text. Longus has chosen a somewhat curious verb with which to suspend the apple from the tree: *epeteto* (3.33) is from *petomai*, the verb 'to fly.' It is generally used of creatures with wings or of emotions that swoop through the heart. Especially frequent of erotic emotion, this verb is used, for example, by Sappho in fr. 31 to say that eros "puts the heart in my chest on wings" or "makes my heart fly." Here Longus puts the verb in the imperfect tense. That is, he stalls the action of the verb in time (the imperfect expresses continuity) so that, like the arrow in Zeno's paradox, the apple flies while standing still. Moreover, the sentence in which the apple flies is a sentence floating in paradoxical, paratactic relation to the sentences before it. The relation is paratactic because the connective joining this sentence to the text is simply and (*kai*). The relation is paradoxical because the statement "and one apple was floating" is a flat contradiction of the three foregoing statements which tell us that the tree had been picked clean, neither fruit nor leaf remained, every single branch was bare. Translators of Longus invariably change his "and" to a "but," so that the impertinent apple darts out suddenly into your grammatical purview from an adversative clause. But Longus' aim is not so ordinary. His grammar intercepts your complacent purview and splits it in half. On the one hand, you see a tree picked bare. On the other hand, an apple floats. *"And"* the relation between them is something paradoxical. Longus' "and" places you at a blind point from which you see more than is literally there.

Longus expects a lot of his reader. The privileged position of knowledge you enjoy as you read *Daphnis and Chloe* does not simply rest on believing things will end well. Longus assumes, and plays upon, the whole history of erotic *topoi* and grammatical acumen available to a literate audience. He wishes to give you a sustained experience of that register of mental activity, metaphor, which best approximates eros. Think how it feels. As you read the novel your mind shifts from the level of characters, episodes and clues to the level of ideas, solutions, exegesis. The activity is delightful, but also one of pain. Each shift is accompanied by a sharp sense that something is being lost, or has already been lost. Exegesis mars and disrupts pure absorption in the narrative. The narrative insists on distracting your attention from exegesis. Yet your mind is unwilling to let go of either level of activity, and remains arrested at a point of stereoscopy between the two. They compose one meaning. The novelist who constructs this moment of emotional and cognitive interception is making love, and you are the object of his wooing. "The book and its author was our pimp!" cries Francesca in hell, or so we read in the *Inferno* (5.137).

Letters, Letters

'Letters' (*grammata*) can mean 'letters of the alphabet' and also 'epistles' in Greek as in English. Novels contain letters of both kinds, and offer two different perspectives on the blind point of desire. Letters in the broad sense, that is to say the floating ruse of the novel as a written text, provide erotic tension on the level of the reading experience. There is a triangular circuit running from the writer to the reader to the characters in the story; when its circuit-points connect, the difficult pleasure of paradox can be felt like an electrification. Letters in the narrower sense, epistles or written messages, function within the plots of various novels as a means of erotic subterfuge between characters. The effect is as you would expect: triangular, paradoxical, electric. In the numerous epistolary scenarios to be found in ancient novels, letters are never used to convey a direct declaration of love between lover and beloved. Letters stand oblique to the action and unfold a three-cornered relation: A writes to C about B, or B reads a letter from C in the presence of A, and so on. When letters are read in novels, the immediate consequence is to inject paradox into lover's emotions (pleasure and pain at once) and into their strategies (now obstructed by an absent presence).

Consider a novel of Achilles Tatius (third-fourth century A.D.) called *Clitophon and Leucippe*. The hero (Clitophon), who believes his beloved (Leucippe) to be dead, is on the point of marrying another woman when he receives a letter from Leucippe. He interrupts the wedding to read Leucippe's letter, which brings her "before the eyes of his soul" and starts a deep blush of shame on his cheek "as if he had been caught in the very act of adultery" (5.19). Clitophon immediately sits down to write a reply "dictated by Eros himself." Its opening lines neatly plot out the three-point circuit connecting lover, beloved and *grammata* in their standard angles:

"Χαῖρέ μοι, ὦ δέσποινα Λευκίππη. δυστυχῶ μὲν ἐν οἷς εὐτυχῶ, ὅτι σὲ παρὼν παροῦσαν ὡς ἀποδημοῦσαν ὁρῶ διὰ γραμμάτων."

"Hail, my lady Leucippe. I am miserable in the midst of joy because I see you present and at the same time absent in your letter." (5.20)

Clitophon goes on in the letter to proclaim his love and entreat Leucippe to maintain her desire until he can unite with her. Written letters have the presence and authority of a third person, who is witness, judge and conduit of erotic charges. Letters are the mechanism of erotic paradox, at once connective and separative, painful and sweet. Letters construct the space of desire and kindle in it those contradictory emotions that keep the lover alert to his own impasse. Letters arrest and complicate an existing two-term situation by conjuring a third person who is not literally there, making suddenly visible the difference between what is (the actual and present erotic relation between Clitophon and the other woman) and what could be (the ideal love of Clitophon and Leucippe). Letters project the ideal on a screen of the actual. From within letters, Eros acts.

A more hieratic example comes from Heliodoros' novel *Aethiopica*. Here the written text is not a letter but functions in the same way. Heliodoros' heroine (Charicleia) is the white-skinned daughter born to the black queen of Ethiopia. The queen elects to abandon her child at birth rather than face the suspicious questions of her husband, and so Charicleia is exposed, wrapped in a *tainia* (fillet or headscarf). No ordinary *tainia*, however: the queen inscribes it with a written text explaining the baby's history and white skin. As it happens the infant is rescued by priests and reared at Delphi. Years pass and the novel is in its fourth book before the novelist discloses to us the text on the *tainia*. The scene of its reading is reserved for a moment of erotic crisis: Charicleia is on the verge of dying of love for a certain Theagenes when the *tainia* is read by a priest who hopes to save her life. The queen of Ethiopia speaks from the *tainia*:

> ... ἐπειδὴ δέ σε λευκὴν ἀπέτεκον, ἀπρόσφυλον Αἰθιόπων χροιὰν ἀπαυγάζουσαν, ἐγὼ μὲν τὴν αἰτίαν ἐγνώριζον, ὅτι μοι παρὰ τὴν ὁμιλίαν τὴν πρὸς τὸν ἄνδρα προσβλέψαι τὴν Ἀνδρομέδαν ἡ γραφὴ παρασχοῦσα, καὶ πανταχόθεν ἐπιδείξασα γυμνήν (ἄρτι γὰρ αὐτὴν ἀπὸ τῶν πετρῶν ὁ Περσεὺς κατῆγεν), ὁμοειδὲς ἐκείνῃ τὸ σπαρὲν οὐκ εὐτυχῶς ἐμόρφωσεν.

... when I gave birth to you with your white skin radiant as light—an incongruous thing in an Ethiopian—I recognized the reason. You see, at the very moment when my husband penetrated me I was staring at a painting of Andromeda. The painting showed her completely naked, just as Perseus was claiming her from the rock. Her likeness changed my seed—not luckily. (4.8.5)

Now here is an interesting triangle. Charicleia's desire for Theagenes unfolds backwards in time to include an aesthetic infidelity on the part of her mother. At the moment of coitus with her husband, the queen was thinking of something else. Her attention was caught by a different love affair, the mythical or ideal eros of Perseus and Andromeda. The queen triangulated. It is not a simple triangle. Heliodoros is not a simple author. One Byzantine critic likened Heliodoros' narrative to a cluster of snakes with tails exposed, heads hidden (Michael Psellos; Colonna 1938, 364). Moreover, Heliodoros warns us in advance that the queen's writing style is recondite, for she chose to inscribe the *tainia*

> ... γράμμασιν Αἰθιοπικοῖς, οὐ δημοτικοῖς ἀλλὰ βασιλικοῖς, ἐστιγμένην, ἃ δὴ τοῖς Αἰγυπτίων ἱερατικοῖς καλουμένοις ὠμοίωνται.

> ... not in the demotic Ethiopian alphabet but in the 'royal' letters [*grammasin basilikois*] which resemble Egyptian hieratic script.　(4.8.1)

The script is precious and the meaning convolute. Nonetheless the familiar components of an erotic triangle are recognizable. We see the king of Ethiopia reaching out to unite with his beloved wife. As he does so, an act of interception occurs, a third angle opens. By a shift of distance from far to near, from ideal to real, Perseus and Andromeda intercept the queen's glance and split her desire. Her imagination leaps. And as her imagination reaches out from actual (husband) to possible (Perseus and Andromeda), something paradoxical happens: Charicleia.

Charicleia is a paradox first on the level of fact (white from black) but also on the level of inference. Although in her own person she has not compromised her love for Theagenes, yet her perfect chastity (of which the white skin might have been thought a symbol) is now seen to have been colored (white) from before her birth by a momentary inconstancy in the mind of her mother. Whiteness is in her case a clue to impurity: you see the sense of this projected on its incongruence, as the *tainia* unfolds its tale. You contemplate that point of incongruent congruence and the data of the reasoning seem to go askew in your mind. Can a painting change real flesh? Can a metaphor turn reality white? It is a delightful story but unsatisfying as an exegesis, and your mind keeps reaching out for an answer. Each time you reach, conception shifts to interception: the black seed of Charicleia folds into the white skin of Andromeda and disappears. Placed at the blind point of that ruse you feel delight and chagrin. Your mixed response is echoed by the reader within the novel. The priest (Calasiris) who reads the *tainia* in hope of discovering how to save Charicleia records his reaction:

> . . . when I read these things, I recognized and marvelled at the economy of the gods and at the same time I was filled with pleasure and pain: I found myself in quite a novel state of mind, weeping and rejoicing simultaneously. (4.9.1)

Let us be clear about the importance Heliodoros has given to reading and writing in this pivotal scene of his novel. Because of the way he has ordered his narrative, it is an act of reading that arrests and complicates the erotic situation (between Charicleia and Theagenes) by unfolding a third angle (the history of Charicleia's conception). At that third angle the ruse of eros operates. Paradox is generated. Emotions divide. From within a written text eros acts upon Calasiris to create in him the state of mind typical of the readers of novels. Into that hieratic text you reach for the meaning of Charicleia's white skin. The meaning shifts, changes and eludes you, but you continue to long to pursue it, as if it were the beloved itself.

We might compare with these Greek novels an anonymous Latin romance of the fifth or sixth century A.D. entitled *History of Apollonius of Tyre*, which relates the love of Apollonius for the daughter of the king of Pentapolis. Apollonius contrives to win the girl by becoming her tutor and distracts her attention from rival suitors with the seductive power of letters themselves. When she falls in love it is with Apollonius' learning, the novelist tells us (ch. 17). Rivals demand audience but her father waves them away:

Rex ait non apto tempore interpellastis. Filia enim
mea studio uacat et pro amore studiorum inbecillis
iacet.

Now is not a good time to press your suit, for my
daughter is entirely absorbed with learning and is
so in love with her studies that she lies ill in bed.
(ch. 19)

King Antiochus then employs the mechanism of letters to
set up an erotic triangle. He invites each suitor to write
down his name and dowry on a tablet, which he will forward to his daughter so that she may choose among
them. Apollonius carries the tablet to her and, as she
stands reading it before him, the familiar triangle of
lover, beloved and rivals-in-writing is marked out. But
this heroine is not unlettered herself. Displeased with the
geometry of the triangle before her, the king's daughter
reshuffles the angles. She writes Apollonius' name on the
tablet and sends it back to her father with her seal (ch.
20-21). Literary critics of the novel are impatient with
this "letter-writing farce" and pose plausible questions
like "Why does the king suggest the extraordinary and
cumbersome procedure of writing letters to someone a
few yards away?" (Perry 1967, 306-307). Do the letters
say anything that could not be said otherwise?

Letters in this romance, as in Heliodoros' novel, be-
speak their own power, a power to change reality eroti-
cally. It is letters that stir the fire of love in the king's
daughter when she meets Apollonius. It is letters that
pose the dilemma of absent presence for lover and beloved when she stands before Apollonius reading out the
names of his rivals. It is letters that permit her to set the
triangle of eros on its head when she reaches through literary convention and rewrites the love scene to suit her
own desire. This heroine understands the erotic art of letters as thoroughly as her own author. As feelingly as
Montaigne's, her Page makes love.

There are two kinds of letters here (alphabet and epistle) and there are two kinds of love being made (as reader, you also are being wooed). Each one fits within the other. As letters of the alphabet compose lovers' epistles, so the love affair of Apollonius and the king's daughter composes the seductive action of this novel. But the page is taken over by the heroine. She commandeers the letters of a particular epistle and constructs for herself the love story that she wishes the novel to tell. By a shift of distance she reaches from within the plot to triangulate that plot (inscribing Apollonius' name among his rivals) as if she herself were the novelist, as if letters themselves were an inescapably erotic form of understanding.

When she makes that shift, the king's daughter does so by an act of imagination, reaching out from actual (the list of suitors named on her father's tablet) to possible (the unnamed suitor of her own preference). When she makes that shift she takes over the letter-writing *topos* from her author, stepping from one (literal) plane of storytelling to a different plane. That shift is an act of lettristic impertinence and it delights you. At the same time you may find the whole procedure of the scene "extraordinary and cumbersome." But by your understanding of letters as a novelistic *topos*, you are pulled into a kinetic, triangular, delightful and disturbing action of eros. As she writes her lover's name on the tablet, the king's daughter seduces you.

Folded Meanings

From the time of its earliest use the technique of writing and reading was appreciated by the ancients as an apparatus of privacy or secrecy. All communication is to some extent public in a society without writing. Certainly a message sent by herald and declaimed in the open air is a less private communiqué than a letter written for your eyes alone to read. Early readers and writers seem to have been intensely aware of this difference. There is an ancient riddle, attributed to Sappho, that expresses their attitude:

> ἔστι φύσις θήλεια βρέφη σῴζουσ᾽ ὑπὸ κόλποις
> αὑτῆς, ὄντα δ᾽ ἄφωνα βοὴν ἵστησι γεγωνὸν
> καὶ διὰ πόντιον οἶδμα καὶ ἠπείρου διὰ πάσης
> οἷς ἐθέλει θνητῶν, τοῖς δ᾽ οὐδὲ παροῦσιν ἀκούειν
> ἔξεστιν, κωφὴν δ᾽ ἀκοῆς αἴσθησιν ἔχουσιν. . . .

What creature is it (Sappho asks) that is female in nature and hides in its womb unborn children who, although they are voiceless, speak to people far away?

Sappho answers the riddle herself:

> θήλεια μέν νύν ἐστι φύσις ἐπιστολή, βρέφη δ᾽ ἐν
> αὑτῇ περιφέρει τὰ γράμματα· ἄφωνα δ᾽ ὄντα ταῦτα
> τοῖς πόρρω λαλεῖ οἷς βούλεθ᾽, ἕτερος δ᾽ ἂν τύχῃ
> τις πλησίον ἑστὼς ἀναγινώσκοντος, οὐκ ἀκούεται.

The female creature is a letter (epistle). The unborn children are the letters (of the alphabet) it carries. And the letters, although they have no voices,

· 98 ·

speak to people far away, whomever they wish. But
if some other person happens to be standing right
beside the one who is reading, he will not
hear. (Antiphanes, *CAF*, fr. 196; Ath. 450c)

Letters make the absent present, and in an exclusive
way, as if they were a private code from writer to reader.
The poet Archilochos applies to his own poetry the metaphor of a code, for he refers to himself, sending off a
poem to someone, as a *skutalē*. Best known as a method
employed by the Spartans for sending despatches, the
skutalē was a staff or baton around which was wound a
roll of leather. This was used as a code simply by wrap-
ping it in a particular way, writing the message across the
result, and then sending the unwound strip to the re-
ceiver, who rewound it on a similar staff to read it (Jeffrey 1961, 57). Archilochos' metaphor understands the
act of communication as an intimate collusion between
writer and reader. They compose a meaning between
them by matching two halves of a text. It is a meaning
not accessible to others.

A well-known passage of Aeschylus' *Suppliants* also
emphasizes the cryptographic possibilities of writing.
Here King Pelasgos, announcing a democratic decision
viva voce, contrasts his own plain and public utterance
with the furtive record of written texts:

τοιάδε δημόπρακτος ἐκ πόλεως μία
ψῆφος κέκρανται, μήποτ᾽ ἐκδοῦναι βίαι
στόλον γυναικῶν· τῶνδ᾽ ἐφήλωται τορῶς
γόμφος διαμπὰξ ὡς μένειν ἀραρότως.
ταῦτ᾽ οὐ πίναξίν ἐστιν ἐγγεγραμμένα
οὐδ᾽ ἐν πτυχαῖς βύβλων κατεσφραγισμένα,
σαφῆ δ᾽ ἀκούεις ἐξ ἐλευθεροστόμου
γλώσσης.

Such is the decree that issues from the city
by unanimous popular vote. . . .

A bolt has been nailed straight through this,
piercingly,
so it stays fixed.
It has not been written on tablets
nor sealed up in the folds of books,
but you hear it plain from a free-speaking
tongue.

(942-49)

Words that are written, Pelasgos implies, may fold away
and disappear. Only the spoken word is not sealed,
folded, occult or undemocratic.

Now folding books and tablets were a reality in the ancient world. The most common writing surface for letters
and messages in archaic and classical times was the *deltos*, a hinged wooden or wax tablet that was folded up on
itself after inscription to conceal the words written
within. The reader unfolded the tablet to confront a
meaning meant only for him. Tablets of metal were also
used for writing, especially by people consulting an oracle. For example at Dodona, active as an oracular sanc-
tuary from the seventh century, archaeologists have un-
covered about one hundred and fifty tablets on which
were written questions for the oracle of Zeus. The great
variety in handwriting, spelling and grammar on the tablets indicates that each was inscribed by the inquirer himself. The tablets are of lead. Each is cut in a narrow band
like a ribbon with writing in two to four lines running the
length of the band. In nearly every instance the band
after writing has been neatly folded several times so as to
conceal the writing inside. This folding was evidently the
reason for the shape of the lead ribbons and also for the
fact that the written inquiry was never carried over to the
reverse of the band (Parke 1967, 114). The words you
write on your lead at Dodona are a secret between you
and the oracle of Zeus.

Folded texts and private meanings were a literal fact

for ancient readers. But there is a metaphorical reality here too. It is a metaphor as old as Homer, whose telling of the Bellerophon myth in *Iliad* 6 is the oldest story we have in Greek about letters, reading and writing.

Bellerophon Is Quite Wrong
After All

Although embedded in an epic genealogy, Bellerophon's is a story of erotic triangles, ideal matter for a novel. We do not know where Homer got the story; presumably it reflects an extremely ancient Lydian layer in the epic tradition from which he drew, dating from a time long before his own (supposing we place Homer in the eighth century B.C.). It was a time when some form of reading and writing was known to the Aegean world, or at least to the people of Lykia where the story is set. No one knows what system of writing this was. Homer himself may not have known. The poet is widely believed by scholars to have been illiterate; in any event, he betrays not the slightest fascination, as he tells his Bellerophon-story, with the phenomenon of writing and reading that figures crucially within it. The motif of letters falls so flat here it makes you wonder.

Bellerophon was a young man gifted by the gods with remarkable beauty (*Il.* 6.156). Exiled from his home for murder, he takes refuge with King Proitos of Ephyra and all unwittingly stirs love in the heart of Anteia, Proitos' wife. The lover is "maddened by desire" (6.160), the beloved unresponsive: a typical erotic scenario, which draws a typical erotic reaction from Anteia. She triangulates. By means of a lying tale she inflames her husband to jealousy of Bellerophon, so that he resolves to destroy the young man, but not in direct encounter. Proitos arranges a kind of deadfall, in which the three angles of eros will close on Bellerophon when actuated by a deadly text. Bellerophon is despatched to Lykia, to the halls of Anteia's father, carrying his own death warrant:

πέμπε δέ μιν Λυκίην δέ, πόρεν δ' ὅ γε σήματα λυγρὰ
γράψας ἐν πίνακι πτυκτῷ θυμοφθόρα πολλά,
δεῖξαι δ' ἠνώγειν ᾧ πενθερῷ ὄφρ' ἀπόλοιτο.

and Proitos sent him to Lykia and bestowed on him a
written text that would kill him [*sēmata lugra*]
for he wrote many life-destroying things
[*thumophthora*] on a folded tablet
and bid him show it to Anteia's father so that he
might be destroyed.
(6.168-70)

What are the "life-destroying things" on the folded tablet? The life to be destroyed is Bellerophon's and the destroyer, Anteia's father. Most likely, then, Proitos relates to the father that his chaste daughter has been shamed by the rapist rogue Bellerophon: the erotic triangle that began in Anteia's imagination now acquires the status of written fact. (That fact is a lie but so is any novel; this should not detain us.) Upon the fact is projected a metaphor that almost kills Bellerophon. The metaphor brings together the action of wooing a lover and the action of reading a written text on the screen of Bellerophon's life. For he is twice unwitting victim of the signs he carries. First his own beauty, gift of the gods, seduces Anteia, unknown to him. Then the folded tablet, bestowed by Proitos, writes the order for his death, and he does not read it. "Life-destroying things" are the text he carries, but the word (*thumophthora*) is an ambiguous one. On the surface, "life-destroying things" refers to the projected murder of Bellerophon, but the adjective can also convey the emotional sense "heartbreaking" (as it does in *Od.* 4.716) and evoke the seductive beauty that drove Anteia mad. Unwitting wooing began Bellerophon's story. Unread writing will end it. These possibilities float just where Bellerophon cannot see them.

Bellerophon is a living metaphor for the blind point of eros, carrying on his face (beauty) and in his hands (tablet) a meaning he does not decode. The text remains for him a folded one, literally and metaphorically. Unfolded, its two sides compose one meaning, a meaning vitally incongruent with the actual fact of Bellerophon (alive). It is a meaning that is a verb and that will act to assign a new predicate to Bellerophon (dead). It is a meaning whose novel sense will not entirely obscure the previous sense, nor the difference between them (for death keeps life visible while making it absent). The meaning is a blind point where Bellerophon's knowledge of his own situation disappears into itself. If Bellerophon were to unfold the tablet and intercept the message he is carrying, he would exclaim (with Aristotle): "Well, I was quite wrong after all!" That would be a moment of wrenching pain. Also it might save his life. We have to keep going back to such moments if we wish to maintain contact with the possible.

"Not anyone else, Bellerophon carried the letter himself: in a so-to-speak tragic manner, caught by his own wings," says Eustathius in his ancient commentary on the Iliadic text. Eustathius is overinterpreting. As Homer tells the story there is nothing tragic about it, for Bellerophon is not "caught" in Lykia at all. After arriving at the court of Anteia's father, he hands over the damning letter to the king, then proceeds to discredit its contents by a few heroic exploits and win the king's other daughter to wife as his reward. The folded tablet is not mentioned again. One can see easily how Bellerophon's tale, told from the point of view of Anteia for instance, could have furnished a tragedy (see Euripides' *Hippolytus*). Equally, there is fair material for weaving a romance around Bellerophon and his Lykian bride. The *Iliad* does not tell these stories. Homer's hero is a warrior and a winner. Love is incidental to him. Moreover, attempts to interpret him symbolically prove frustrating. Bellerophon wins out in the end by heroic virtue, not by unfolding his own metaphor. Homer is not primarily interested in the puzzles of inference and reference that amuse novelists and later poets; he has a war to wage. Nor is Homer interested in the writing on the folded tablet. Like Bellerophon, he transmits and ignores it. Why does Bellerophon not read the tablet? Has he no curiosity? Is he illiterate? Does he scruple to break the seal? These same questions might be put to Homer. What is his relation, as a poet speaking from within an ancient oral tradition, to this Lykian vignette about alphabets and love triangles? Can he read the signs he is using?

I do not know how one could answer these questions. A powerful metaphorical potential seems to be fossilized within this traditional story of Bellerophon and his killing text but, except in overinterpretation, it cannot be drawn out. Nonetheless, the story offers some matter for speculation about literacy and its effects on writers and readers. Bellerophon's myth derives, as we have said, from a time when Lykian society knew some form of writing. The myth brings together a number of the notions we have been exploring in ancient novels. For example it is a love story where eros acts from a folded text; its erotic situation includes two terms until the lover deliberately complicates these by adding a third angle; a written text is the mechanism of the complication; along the angle where the written text enters the story move elements of metaphor, inference, paradox and imaginative action; these elements inscribe a blind point at the center of the story and at the center of its hero, Bellerophon; into the blind point we watch several important questions about Bellerophon, and about Homer, disappear.

Can anything be learned from the repeated confluence, in different genres, of these elements with the phenomenon of literacy?

It would seem to make sense that when an author begins to use and to think about reading and writing his imagination is trained along certain lines, his mental landscape is lit from a certain angle. The novel as a genre evolved in adaptation to that angle. Deep within the Bellerophon story some pre-Homeric imagination has traced the same angle. It provides us with a special, intractable pleasure as we read. Homer does not, in the self-conscious manner of the novelists, exploit that pleasure, yet our reading of his version brings us somewhat closer to the question that lies at the heart of the matter.

It is a question about the relations between readers and their reading. We have already recalled the famous words of Francesca in Dante's *Inferno*. Other, similar scenarios come to mind, for example, that of Pushkin's heroine in *Eugene Onegin*:

> Tatiana is besotted by romantic fiction:
> with what attention she now
> reads a delicious novel,
> with what vivid enchantment
> drinks the seductive fiction!
>
> . . . sighs, and having made her own
> another's ecstasy, another's melancholy,
> she whispers in a trance, by heart,
> a letter to the amiable hero.
>   (3:9)

Readers in real life, as well as within fiction, bear witness to the allure of the written text. The novelist Eudora Welty says of her mother: "She read Dickens in the spirit in which she would have eloped with him" (1984, 17). Dickens himself would not have been discomfited by such a spirit in a reader, if we may judge from a letter he wrote to Maria Beadnell in 1855. Here he speaks of his novel *David Copperfield* to the woman who inspired Dora: "Perhaps you have once or twice laid down that book and thought 'How dearly that boy must have loved me and how vividly this man remembers it!'" (Slater 1983, 66). Through Francesca, through Tatiana, through Maria Beadnell, through Eudora Welty's mother, some current of eros leapt from a written page. You have felt it yourself, reading Montaigne or Heliodoros or Sappho. Can we arrive at a more realistic appraisal of this phenomenon? Just what is erotic about reading and writing?

Realist

No one contradicts me now and the salt has gone out of
my life.

Queen Victoria,
after Albert's death

Eros loves strife and delights in paradoxical outcomes.

Chariton, *Chaereas and Callirrhoe* 1.1

It is nothing new to say that all utterance is erotic in some
sense, that all language shows the structure of desire at
some level. Already in Homer's usage, the same verb
(*mnaomai*) has the meaning 'to give heed, to make mention' and also the meaning 'to court, woo, be a suitor.'
Already in ancient Greek myth, the same goddess
(Peithō) has charge of rhetorical persuasion and the arts
of seduction. Already in earliest metaphor, it is 'wings' or
'breath' that move words from speaker to listener as they
move eros from lover to beloved. But words that are
written or read place in sharp, sudden focus the edges of
the units of language and the edges of those units called
'reader' and 'writer.' Back and forth across the edges
moves a symbolic intercourse. As the vowels and consonants of an alphabet interact symbolically to make a certain written word, so writer and reader bring together
two halves of one meaning, so lover and beloved are
matched together like two sides of one knucklebone. An
intimate collusion occurs. The meaning composed is private and true and makes permanent, perfect sense. Ide-
ally speaking, at least, that is the case.

In fact, neither reader nor writer nor lover achieves such consummation. The words we read and the words we write never say exactly what we mean. The people we love are never just as we desire them. The two *symbola* never perfectly match. Eros is in between.

Both the experience of desire and the experience of reading have something to teach us about edges. We have endeavored to see what that is by consulting ancient literature, lyric and romantic, for its exposition of eros. We have watched how archaic poets shape love poems (as triangles) and how ancient novelists construct novels (as a sustained experience of paradox). We caught sight of a similar outline, even in Homer, where the phenomenon of reading and writing surfaces in Bellerophon's story. We speculated about writers' purposes (to seduce readers?) and we are finally led to suspect that what the reader wants from reading and what the lover wants from love are experiences of very similar design. It is a necessarily triangular design, and it embodies a reach for the unknown.

Desire for knowledge is the mark of the beast: Aristotle says "All men reach out to know" (*Metaph.A.* 1.980a21). As you perceive the edge of yourself at the moment of desire, as you perceive the edges of words from moment to moment in reading (or writing), you are stirred to reach beyond perceptible edges—toward something else, something not yet grasped. The unplucked apple, the beloved just out of touch, the meaning not quite attained, are desirable objects of knowledge. It is the enterprise of eros to keep them so. The unknown must remain unknown or the novel ends. As all paradoxes are, in some way, paradoxes *about* paradox, so all eros is, to some degree, desire *for* desire.

Hence, ruses. What is erotic about reading (or writing) is the play of imagination called forth in the space between you and your object of knowledge. Poets and novelists, like lovers, touch that space to life with their metaphors and subterfuges. The edges of the space are the edges of the things you love, whose inconcinnities make your mind move. And there is Eros, nervous realist in this sentimental domain, who acts out of a love of paradox, that is as he folds the beloved object out of sight into a mystery, into a blind point where it can float known and unknown, actual and possible, near and far, desired and drawing you on.

Ice-pleasure

We cannot really say that time 'is' except in virtue of its
continual tendency not to be.

Augustine, *Confessions* 11.14.17

Time watches from the shadow
And coughs when you would kiss.

W. H. Auden, "One Evening"

The blind point of Eros is a paradox in time as well as in
space. A desire to bring the absent into presence, or to
collapse far and near, is also a desire to foreclose then
upon now. As lover you reach forward to a point in time
called 'then' when you will bite into the long-desired apple. Meanwhile you are aware that as soon as 'then' su-
pervenes upon 'now,' the bittersweet moment, which is
your desire, will be gone. You cannot want that, and yet
you do. Let us see what this feels like.

Below is a fragment of a satyr play by Sophokles entitled *The Lovers of Achilles*. The fragment is a description
of desire. It turns eros subtly, permitting different aspects
of its perversity to come to light. At the center is a cold,
original pleasure. Around the center move circles of time,
different kinds of time, different dilemmas set by time.
Notice that this poem is an analogy. Neither its pleasure
nor its various kinds of time are to be identified with
eros, but the way they intersect may feel like eros to you.

τὸ γὰρ νόσημα τοῦτ᾽ ἐφίμερον κακόν·
ἔχοιμ᾽ ἂν αὐτὸ μὴ κακῶς ἀπεικάσαι.

ὅταν πάγου φανέντος αἰθρίου χεροῖν
κρύσταλλον ἁρπάσωσι παῖδες εὐπαγῆ,
τὰ πρῶτ᾽ ἔχουσιν ἡδονὰς ποταινίους·
τέλος δ᾽ ὁ θυμὸς οὔθ᾽ ὅπως ἀφῇ θέλει
οὔτ᾽ ἐν χεροῖν τὸ κτῆμα σύμφορον μένειν.
οὕτω δὲ τοὺς ἐρῶντας αὑτὸς ἵμερος
δρᾶν καὶ τὸ μὴ δρᾶν πολλάκις προίεται.

This disease is an evil bound upon the day.
Here's a comparison—not bad, I think:
when ice gleams in the open air,
children grab.
Ice-crystal in the hands is
at first a pleasure quite novel.
But there comes a point—
you can't put the melting mass down,
you can't keep holding it.
Desire is like that.
Pulling the lover to act and not to act,
again and again, pulling.
(fr. 149 Radt)[9]

Much is left unsaid in this poem, as in any formulation of
desire, yet you may feel you know exactly what is meant.
No direct reference is made, for example, to desire as desirable. Here desire is a "disease" and an "evil" from the
first line. Within the comparison (ll. 2-7) desire turns out
to be pleasurable, but its pleasure is that of holding ice in
your hands. An acutely painful pleasure, one would
think, yet again no direct mention is made of the pain-
fulness of ice. Here ice gives a novel kind of enjoyment.

[9] Not inadvertently, the first line of the translation departs from
Radt's emended text (*ephimeron*) in favor of the MS reading (*ephēmeron*). Since Arsenius, the codices' *ephēmeron* ("bound upon the day")
has been changed to *ephimeron* ("lovely, desirable") on alleged
grounds of sense: Why would Sophokles begin his description of
desire by binding it into time? I believe, and hope to show, that it makes compelling sense. *Ephēmeron* is the evil with which we must begin.

The absence of these predictable attributes of ice and of desire surprises you, like a missing step, but you climb on through the poem anyway. And suddenly you find yourself on a staircase rendered by Escher or Piranesi. It goes two places at once and you seem to be standing in both of them. How does that happen?

At first the poem looks like a simple ring composition, for the whole structure is a simile whose *comparandum* (desire, ll. 1 and 8) neatly encircles its *comparatio* (grabbing a handful of ice, ll. 2-7). So, desire forms a ring around the small universe of its victims: the poet who strives to represent it, the children fascinated by its analog, the lover pinned in its compulsion. But that universe does not form the outer circle of the poem. You keep climbing, for the staircase continues to spiral. The desire at the beginning of the poem is desire as transience—it is an "ephemeral evil" (*ephēmeron kakon*), bound to the day that flickers over it. The desire at the end of the poem is desire as repetition—exerting its pull "over and over again" (*pollakis*). So time forms a ring around desire. Now, as you peer down through concentric circles of time, you see at the heart of the poem a piece of ice, melting. The startling likeness of ice drops into your perception with a shock like what the children must feel in their hands. The poem places you for shock, at an interface between two kinds of time, each of which spirals with its own logic upward through the structure of the poem, and through the psychology of desire. They seem to fit one within the other, yet there is a point where the perspectives become incompatible.

The desire for ice is an affair of the moment, transparently. But not only physical time threatens it: here ice-pleasure is a *novelty*. A pleasure "quite novel" says the poet, using an adjective (*potainios*) that is applied by other poets to an innovative scheme (Bacchylides 16.51), an original and unexpected form of torture (Aesch. *PV* 102), a bizarre clattering sound not heard before (Aesch.

Sept. 239). The adjective denotes something fresh and untried, perhaps newfangled. With this adjective Sophokles realigns your sensibility to ice and makes clear that he wishes to depict eros, not just as a difficulty, but as a paradox. Ice, as physical substance, cannot be said to be delightful *because* it melts; but if "melting" is itself a metaphor for the aesthetic consideration of novelty, a paradox begins to come into focus. Novelties, by definition, are short-lived. If ice-pleasure consists, to some degree, in novelty, then ice must melt in order to be desirable.

So as you watch the ice melt, your solicitude for it is distracted by a different kind of care. The ice may lose favor even before it changes state. Its "pleasure" may cease to be "quite novel" and so cease to be pleasure. Suddenly here the laws of physics, which govern events like melting ice, are intersected by certain vaguer psychological laws governing our human enslavement to novelty in moods and styles. Novelty is an affair of the mind and emotions; melting is a physical fact. Each is measured out on a scale that we call temporal, although two different kinds of time are involved. Where does the dilemma of a novelty intercept that of a piece of ice? What should a lover want from time? If you run backwards down the staircase of a day, can you make novelty grow? Or freeze desire?

Let us be subtle about how Sophokles contrives to draw us into these questions. The simile of ice is a delicate and insidious mechanism. It sets up a condition of suspense at the center of the poem that pulls our minds and emotions, as well as our senses, into conflict. We hang upon the physical fate of the melting ice; it is, in a way, the protagonist of the simile and we are watching it perish. At the same time, we care for the hands of the children. Ice is cold and the longer you hold it, the colder your hands get. But this care reminds us of another. The longer you hold it, the more it melts. So would it not be more reasonable to put the ice down, sparing hands and ice? But holding onto ice delights children, for that is a novelty. At this point in our reasoning, time coughs from the shadow, as Auden says. Time is the condition of delightfulness and of perishing both. Time brings the nature of ice into fatal conjuncture with human nature, so that at a critical moment the crystal glamor of ice and the human susceptibility to novelty intersect. One kind of time (that of aesthetic events) intersects another (the time . of physical events) and dislocates it.

Our suspense has a sensual side as well. Sophokles' image of time is a piece of ice melting. It is an image selected not only for its dramatic and melodramatic potential but for its history. As readers of Greek lyric poetry we recognize here a familiar erotic *topos*, for the poets frequently imagine desire to be a sensation of heat and an action of melting. Eros is traditionally "the melter of limbs" (*lusimelēs*). One vivid example from many of this conventional imagery is a fragment from Pindar:

ἀλλ᾽ ἐγὼ τᾶς ἕκατι κηρὸς ὣς δαχθεὶς ἕλᾳ
ἱρᾶν μελισσᾶν τάκομαι, εὖτ᾽ ἂν ἴδω
παίδων νεόγυιον ἐς ἥβαν·

. . . but I am like wax of sacred bees
like wax as the heat bites in:
I melt whenever I look at the fresh limbs of boys.
(Snell-Maehler, fr. 123.10-12)

Conventionally, as we see from Pindar, to melt is in some degree desirable, its context one of delicious heat. Sophokles subverts the image. As we watch his melting ice, all our conventional responses to the melting experience of desire are dislocated. As a conventional lover, you relish the sensation of melting, in your bittersweet way. As an observer of ice, your feelings about melting are different, more complex. You can almost bring those feelings into focus against the screen of the conventional image, but not quite. Eros is in between. Eros' connection with the conventional image of melting, and at the same time with this novel image of it, pulls your mind into vertigo.

Sophokles pulls you, in vertigo, back to the problem of time. His simile unfolds as a paradox of sensations: the uneasy image of hot ice almost comes into focus. The simile involves you in a conflicted response: to save the ice, you must freeze desire. You cannot want that, and yet you do.

Sophokles pulls you, in time, back to the problem of the blind point. Time encircles desire in this poem and the melting ice is an image of the way desire rotates within time. It rotates on an axis of ephemerality: contingent upon the day (*ephēmeron*) it will melt with the day. But days recur. It rotates on an axis of novelty: as lover you are pulled into vertigo "over and over again." You cannot want that, and yet you do. It is quite new every time.

There are different kinds of knowledge, Heisenberg has demonstrated, that cannot be held simultaneously in the mind (for example, the position of a particle and its velocity). The likeness of desire to ice in Sophokles' poem pulls you into such knowledge, a pull that splits your mental vision, much as the lover is split by the paradox of desire. Your moment of stereoscopy on the staircase, as you try to understand this poem, is no bad imitation of that erotic division. A while before Heisenberg, Sophokles appears to have recognized that you can only go so far into thinking about time, or about desire. There comes a point where dilemmas arise, staircases reverse: Eros.

Now Then

Endlessly I sustain the discourse of the beloved's absence; actually a preposterous situation; the other is absent as referent, present as allocutory. This singular distortion generates a kind of insupportable present; I am wedged between two tenses, that of the reference and that of the allocution: you have gone (which I lament), you are here (since I am addressing you). Whereupon I know what the present, that difficult tense, is: a pure portion of anxiety.

Roland Barthes, *A Lover's Discourse*

The experience of eros is a study in the ambiguities of time. Lovers are always waiting. They hate to wait; they love to wait. Wedged between these two feelings, lovers come to think a great deal about time, and to understand it very well, in their perverse way.

Desire seems to the lover to demolish time in the instant when it happens, and to gather all other moments into itself in unimportance. Yet, simultaneously, the lover perceives more sharply than anyone else the difference between the 'now' of his desire and all the other moments called 'then' that line up before and after it. One of those moments called 'then' contains his beloved. That moment pulls at his attention, vertiginously, by love and hate at once: we can feel something like this vertigo in the poem of Sophokles about melting ice. The lover's real desire, as we see in that handful of ice, is to elude the certainties of physics and float in the ambiguities of a space-time where absent is present and 'now' can include 'then' without ceasing to be 'now.' From his special vantage point "wedged between two tenses" as Barthes says, the lover looks at 'now' and 'then' with a calculating eye and a sinking heart. How he would love to control time! Instead, time controls him.

Or rather, Eros makes use of time to control the lover. The lover in Greek poetry views with singular candor and a degree of irony his own subjection to time. He sees himself pinned in an impossible double bind, victim of novelty and of recurrence at once. There is one very clear sign, throughout the Greek lyric poets, that these authors were concerned with the perversities of time. It consists of a single word which itself presents, in microcosm, the temporal dilemma of eros. It is the adverb *dēute*. No one who reads Greek lyric poetry can fail to be struck by the frequency and poignancy with which this adverb is used. The poets of love prefer it to any other designation of time (cf. Alkman fr. 59(a)1; Sappho, *LP*, frs. 1.15, 16, 18; 22.11; 83.4; 99.23; 127; 130.1; Anakreon, 349.1; 356(a)6; 356(b)1; 358; 371.1; 376.1; 394(b); 400.1; 401.1; 412; 413.1; 428.1 *PMG*). What point in time does *dēute* denote?

The adverb represents a '*crasis*' or 'mingling' of two words that have been contracted into one for euphonic reasons. *Crasis* is a common phenomenon in Greek, but *crasis* in this case produces an uncommonly stereoscopic effect: each of the two words that make up *dēute* has a different vantage point on time. Their intersection creates something of a paradox.

Deute combines the particle *dē* with the adverb *aute*. The particle *dē* signifies vividly and dramatically that something is actually taking place at the moment (Denniston 1954, 203, 219, 250). The adverb *aute* means 'again, once again, over again' (LSJ). The particle *dē* marks a lively perception in the present moment: 'Look at that now!' The adverb *aute* peers past the present moment to a pattern of repeated actions stretching behind it: 'Not for the first time!' *Dē* places you in time and emphasizes that placement: *now*. *Aute* intercepts 'now' and binds it into a history of *'thens'*.

A complex word like *dēute* can create a complex tone. A note of powerful, alert emotion is struck by the particle *dē* itself, which can waken a range of overtones from urgent pathos through various degrees of scorn. Some shade of irony or skepticism is often noticeable (Denniston 1954, 203-206). This is a word on which the eyes open wide in sudden perception, then narrow in understanding. The adverb *aute* closes over that understanding like two hands joined in acquiescence, with a deep nod: again and again.

When the lyric poets insert *dēute* in their love poems, what is its effect? Let us consider first an example with which we are already familiar. We began this essay with a fragment of Sappho (*LP*, fr. 130):

Ἔρος δηὖτέ μ᾽ ὁ λυσιμέλης δόνει,
γλυκύπικρον ἀμάχανον ὄρπετον

Eros—here it goes again! [*dēute*]—the limbloosener
   whirls me,
sweetbitter, impossible to fight off, creature stealing
   up

The untranslatable adverb *dēute* comes like one long, rather wild sigh at the beginning of the poem, as the lover perceives her attacker and understands that it is (oh no!) already too late (not again!) to avoid desire. In another poem Sappho addresses a lover and says:

.]. ε .[. . . .].[. . .κ]έλομαι σ.[
. .]. γυλα.[. . .]ανθι λάβοισα α.[
. .]κτιν, ἆς σε δηὖτε πόθος τ.[
ἀμφιπόταται
τὰν κάλαν· ἀ γὰρ κατάγωγις αὖτα[
ἐπτόαις᾽ ἴδοισαν,

... I bid you take your [lyre] and sing of [Gongyla]
while desire flies round you again now [*dēute*]
for her dress made you
lose your breath when you saw it ...
(*LP*, fr. 22.9-13).

The Spartan poet Alkman gives us this example:

Ἔρως με δηὖτε Κύπριδος Ϝέκατι
γλυκὺς κατείβων καρδίαν ἰαίνει.

Eros—yes again! [*dēute*]—for Kyrpris' sake
the sweet one is melting me down,
is making my heart grow warm
(fr. 59(a) *PMG*).

Each of these poems is a stark evocation of the present
moment intersected by an echo from the past. The lover
who can stand apart from her own experience and assess
it in these terms is one who has learned to take up a certain vantage point on time, telescoping 'then' upon
'now.' Sappho is adept at doing so, as are the other lyric
poets of this period. The technique gives their poems an
unusual force, as moments cut out of real time. How did
they come to evolve this technique?

These poets so fascinated by the perversities of time
were probably, I believe, among the first Greeks to ab-
sorb and employ skills of reading and writing in their poetic composition. Literacy can make a difference to one's
view of time. Let us consider how.

We habitually describe time in metaphors of passage.
Time passes. Time is a stream that flows past, a track that
unwinds, a road down which we walk. All our events
and actions and utterances are part of the passage of
time. Language, especially, is embedded in this moving
process and the words we speak are gone when the time
is gone—"on wings" as Homer says. "Language if
grasped in its true nature is constantly and at every moment transient" (Humboldt 1848, 6:8). An act of speech,

then, is an experience of temporal process: when you pronounce the word 'transient,' the second syllable is not present until the first has ceased to be (cf. Augustine, *Confessions* 11.27). An act of reading and writing, on the other hand, is an experience of temporal arrest and manipulation. As writer or reader you stand on the edge of transience, and hear from the shadows the sound of an ambiguous cough. The word 'transient' stares back at you from the page, poignant as a piece of melting ice. And it does not pass away. Temporally, the word stands to you in a somewhat perverse relation, permanent and transient at once as it is. Mastery of this relation is part of the study of letters. It gives the reader or writer a taste of what it would be like to control time.

When you read or write you seem to achieve that control which the lover craves: a vantage point from which the dilemmas of 'now' and 'then' may be viewed with detachment. When desire is the subject of a text you are reading, you can open it anywhere and end when you like. If Eros is something written on a page, you can close the book and be shut of him. Or go back and reread the words again and again. A piece of ice melts forever there. What is written in letters "stays immovable and remains the same" says the fifth-century orator Isokrates (*Against the Sophists* 12). Plato ponders the matter of writers and their attitude to writing in his *Phaedrus*. "Writing has this strange power," he says: people who learn the art of letters come to believe in their own ability to render things "clear and fixed" for all time (*Phdr.* 275c; cf. 277d). It can be a dangerous belief. For it would be a remarkable power.

What difference would such power make to someone in love? What would the lover ask of time if he were in control? These are questions relevant to our investigation of eros since, in general, we are trying to see what the passion of love has to teach us about reality. And love is an issue of control. What does it mean to control another human being? to control oneself? to lose control? The ancient poets provide data for answering such questions in their descriptions of desire. The philosophers go beyond description. If we follow these questions through the poets to Plato we come, in his *Phaedrus*, to a prescription of what the lover should ask of love and of time and of control itself. The prescription is especially interesting to us because Plato projects these questions upon philosophic worry about the nature of reading and writing.

Why do reading and writing worry Plato? His worry seems closely tied to "this strange power" that writing has. Delusion resides within it, a delusion persuasive enough to be worrisome because it is introduced into the soul of a reader or writer by a mechanism he cannot resist: Eros. Sokrates' interlocutor in the *Phaedrus* is a young man who has fallen in love with a written text. As Phaedrus and Sokrates talk about that love, in the course of the dialogue, they unfold a blind point where lovers and letters intersect. It is a point in time, as well as in space, for Plato formulates his worry specifically in the light of our mortal situation in time. If we focus on this blind point, the question of control may begin to come into focus.

Erotikos Logos

More happy love! more happy, happy love!

John Keats, "Ode on a Grecian Urn"

Phaedrus is in love with a text composed by the sophist
Lysias. It is an "erotic *logos*" (227c), the written version
of a speech delivered by Lysias on the subject of love. Its
thesis is a deliberately repugnant one. Lysias argues that
a beautiful boy would do better to bestow his favors on
a man who is *not* in love with him than on a man who is
in love with him, and he enumerates the ways in which a
nonlover is preferable to a lover as erotic partner. Desire
stirs Phaedrus when he gazes at the words of this text
(*epethumei*, 228b) and visible joy animates him as he
reads it aloud to Sokrates (234d). Phaedrus treats the
text as if it were his *paidika* or beloved boy, Sokrates observes (236b) and uses it as a tool of seduction, to draw
Sokrates beyond the city limits for an orgy of reading in
the open countryside (230d-e; cf. 234d). The reading
elicits from Sokrates an admission that he himself is a
"lover of *logos*" (*andri philologō*, 236e; cf. *tōn logōn
erastou*, 228c). *Eros* and *logos* are fitted together in the
Phaedrus as closely as two halves of a knucklebone. Let
us see what meaning is being composed.

The Sidestep

Lysias' speech is designed to alarm standard sentiment and displace preconceptions about love. It aims to be powerfully, seductively subversive. Yet the speech is simple, for it owes all its insights and shock value to one mechanism: Lysias takes up a particular vantage point on time. It is this temporal point of view which differentiates all that a nonlover feels and thinks and does from what a lover feels, thinks or does. It is a point of view that no one who is in love could tolerate. Lysias looks at a love affair from the point of view of the end.

No one in love really believes love will end. Lovers float in that "pure portion of anxiety," the present indicative of desire. They are astonished when they fall in love, they are equally astonished when they fall out of love. This attitude is simply fatuous, in Lysias' view, and must be dispensed with by anyone who would make a realistic appraisal of erotic experience. Lysias insists on one fact, the invariably transient nature of erotic desire, and from this fact his subversive theory of eros devolves.

The relation of desire to time, then, is the fulcrum of Lysias' argument. As soon as the lover's desire flags, Lysias predicts, the lover will lose interest in his beloved boy and exit, with pain and embarrassment all round. He will repudiate the relationship, regret his investment in it and move on to new infatuations. Love based on the physical passion of the moment cannot but falter when that thrill is gone (233a-b). The nonlove of the nonlover, in contrast, having no special commitment to pleasure in the present, can take a consistently atemporal attitude to his love object and to the love affair. 'Now' and 'then' are moments of equal value to the nonlover. So he says to the boy he is courting:

... πρῶτον μὲν οὐ τὴν παροῦσαν ἡδονὴν θεραπεύων συνέσομαί σοι, ἀλλὰ καὶ τὴν μέλλουσαν ὠφελίαν ἔσεσθαι, οὐχ ὑπ᾽ ἔρωτος ἡττώμενος ἀλλ᾽ ἐμαυτοῦ κρατῶν, οὐδὲ διὰ σμικρὰ ἰσχυρὰν ἔχθραν ἀναιρούμενος ἀλλὰ διὰ μεγάλα βραδέως ὀλίγην ὀργὴν ποιούμενος, τῶν μὲν ἀκουσίων συγγνώμην ἔχων, τὰ δὲ ἑκούσια πειρώμενος ἀποτρέπειν· ταῦτα γάρ ἐστι φιλίας πολὺν χρόνον ἐσομένης τεκμήρια.

... When I spend time with you I shall not primarily be cultivating the pleasure of the moment but, really, the profit coming in the future, since I am not overthrown by desire but in full control of myself. ... These things are indications of a friendship that will last for a long time. (233b-c)

The consistency of his own outlook permits the nonlover to accommodate change in the beloved, Lysias goes on to argue. The nonlover will not be appalled when his boy's physical appearance changes with age (234b) nor will he endeavor to prevent the boy from changing in other ways, for example, by acquiring new friends, new ideas or assets (232b-d). He will not desert the relationship when passion cools nor begrudge his beloved any of the benefits of friendship, even after the boy's beauty has passed its peak (234b):

ὡς ἐκείνοις μὲν τότε μεταμέλει ὧν ἂν εὖ ποιήσωσιν, ἐπειδὰν τῆς ἐπιθυμίας παύσωνται· τοῖς δὲ οὐκ ἔστι χρόνος ἐν ᾧ μεταγνῶναι προσήκει.

For lovers regret their good services as soon as their desire ceases, but there is no time when it is appropriate for nonlovers to regret. (231a)

"There is no time when" desire is pain for the nonlover. 'Now' and 'then' are for him interchangeable: his love affair is a series of events in time that can be entered at any point or rearranged in any order without damage to the whole. Lysias' thought process begins from the termination of desire and his text runs eros backwards. Or, as Sokrates puts it:

οὐδὲ ἀπ᾽ ἀρχῆς ἀλλ᾽ ἀπὸ τελευτῆς ἐξ ὑπτίας ἀνά-
παλιν διανεῖν ἐπιχειρεῖ τὸν λόγον, καὶ ἄρχεται
ἀφ᾽ ὧν πεπαυμένος ἂν ἤδη ὁ ἐραστὴς λέγοι πρὸς τὰ
παιδικά.

... he does not begin at the beginning but tries to swim backwards against the current of the *logos*, starting from the end. He begins with what the lover would say to his boy when the affair was over. (264a)

Lysias sidesteps the whole dilemma of eros in one move. It is a move in time: he simply declines to enter the moment that is 'now' for the man in love, the present moment of desire. Instead, he stations himself safely at an imaginary 'then' and looks back upon desire from a vantage point of emotional disengagement. He is able to include, in his appraisal of the erotic situation 'now,' all the likelihoods and implications of the same erotic situation 'then.' Lysias does not create a stereoscopic image out of these two points in time, pulling your perceptions askew as Sophokles does in the poem about melting ice. Lysias' 'now' and 'then' are not discontinuous or incompatible with one another, and their convergence is not paintful or paradoxical for the nonlover: desire is invested at neither point. Eros traditionally puts the lover in the position of genuinely desiring both points at once. Lysias' erotic theory forestalls this problem. The nonlover is unlikely ever to find himself staring down in desperation at a lump of melting ice. When this man picks up ice it is in full expectation that he will soon have a handful of cold water. He likes cold water fine. And he has no *special* affection for ice.

Such is the substance of Lysias' speech. When Phaedrus finishes reading it aloud, he solicits Sokrates' opinion and Sokrates confesses himself somewhat dissatisfied with the *logos* as a rhetorical production (234e). He seems to recall that the same topics have been treated:

> ... ἤ που Σαπφοῦς τῆς καλῆς ἤ Ἀνακρέοντος τοῦ σοφοῦ ἤ καὶ συγγραφέων τινῶν.

> ... by the beautiful Sappho, I think, or the wise Anakreon or even by some prose writers.... (235c).

Whereupon he undertakes to expound a form of the Lysian thesis himself. Sokrates' speech admits and restates Lysias' emphasis on the temporal factor. He agrees with Lysias that a very important question to ask, in any evaluation of erotic experience, is 'What does the lover want from time?' He further agrees that what the conventional lover wants is to remain in the 'now' of desire at any cost, even to the extent of radically damaging and deforming his beloved in order to do so. Such a lover, Sokrates says, will stunt the growth of his beloved in every direction that leads the boy away from direct dependence on his *erastēs*. He will inhibit the boy from normal physical development in outdoor life, keeping him in shadow and cosmetics, away from manly toils (239c-d). He will set up similar barriers to the boy's cultural and intellectual development, lest the *paidika* grow beyond him in mind:

> φθονερὸν δὴ ἀνάγκη εἶναι, καὶ πολλῶν μὲν ἄλλων
> συνουσιῶν ἀπείργοντα καὶ ὠφελίμων ὅθεν ἂν
> μάλιστ' ἀνὴρ γίγνοιτο, μεγάλης αἴτιον εἶναι
> βλάβης, μεγίστης δὲ τῆς ὅθεν ἂν φρονιμώτατος εἴη·
> τοῦτο δὲ ἡ θεία φιλοσοφία τυγχάνει ὄν, ἧς ἐραστὴν
> παιδικὰ ἀνάγκη πόρρωθεν εἴργειν, περίφοβον ὄντα
> τοῦ καταφρονηθῆναι· τά τε ἄλλα μηχανᾶσθαι ὅπως
> ἂν ᾖ πάντα ἀγνοῶν καὶ πάντα ἀποβλέπων εἰς τὸν
> ἐραστήν.

The lover is of necessity jealous and will do great
damage to his beloved, restricting him from many
advantageous associations which would do most to
make a man of him, and especially from that which
would bring his intellect to its capacity—that is, divine philosophy. The lover will have to keep his boy
far away from philosophy, because of his enormous
fear of being despised. And he will contrive to keep
him ignorant of everything else as well, so the boy
looks to his lover for everything. (239b-c)

Finally, this lover will discourage his *paidika* from at-
taining an adult life in society:

ἔτι τοίνυν ἄγαμον, ἄπαιδα, ἄοικον ὅτι πλεῖστον
χρόνον παιδικὰ ἐραστὴς εὔξαιτ᾽ ἂν γενέσθαι, τὸ
αὑτοῦ γλυκὺ ὡς πλεῖστον χρόνον καρποῦσθαι
ἐπιθυμῶν.

Furthermore the lover would fervently wish his beloved to remain without marriage, child, or house-
hold for as long a time as possible, since it is his desire to reap the fruit that is sweet to himself for as
long a time as possible. (240a)

In sum, this harmful lover does not want his beloved boy
to grow up. He prefers to stop time.

Sokrates and Lysias agree, then, that an *erastēs* of the
conventional type damages his beloved in the course of
loving him. They also agree on the instrument of damage, namely an attempt to control time. What this lover
asks of time is the power to stall his *paidika* at the *akmē*
of boyhood, in a timeless status quo of dependence upon
his *erastēs*. The boy makes himself desirable by willing-
ness to be arrested in time in this way. Sokrates' description of this boy and his dilemma makes him sound somewhat like the piece of melting ice in Sophokles' poem:

. . . οἷος ὢν τῷ μὲν ἥδιστος, ἑαυτῷ δὲ βλαβερώτατος
ἂν εἴη.

. . . as such the boy is most delightful to his lover just
where he does most damage to himself.   (239c)

Damage to the Living

Damage is the subject of this dialogue. Plato is concerned with two sorts of damage. One is the damage done by lovers in the name of desire. The other is the damage done by writing and reading in the name of communication. Why does he set these two sorts of damage beside one another? Plato appears to believe that they act on the soul in analogous ways and violate reality by the same kind of misapprehension. The action of eros does harm to the beloved when the lover takes a certain controlling attitude, an attitude whose most striking feature is its determination to freeze the beloved in time. It is not hard to see that a similar controlling attitude is available to the reader or writer, who sees in written texts the means to fix words permanently outside the stream of time. Isokrates' remark about the immovable sameness of the written letter (*Against the Sophists*, 12) is an indication that this view appealed to ancient writers. Sokrates addresses the view, and its misapprehension, in the concluding section of the *Phaedrus*. He also comments on it indirectly throughout the dialogue by means of various maneuvers of language and staging. Let us consider first Sokrates' explicit assessment of the value of the written word.

Toward the end of the *Phaedrus* he turns from specific speeches to a more general inquiry:

Οὐκοῦν, ὅπερ νῦν προυθέμεθα σκέψασθαι, τὸν λόγον ὅπῃ καλῶς ἔχει λέγειν τε καὶ γράφειν καὶ ὅπῃ μή, σκεπτέον.

We should then examine the theory [*logos*] of what makes speaking or writing good, what makes them bad. (259e)

Comparison of the spoken and written word follows and writing is seen to be mainly useful as a mnemonic device:

πολλῆς ἂν εὐηθείας γέμοι καὶ τῷ ὄντι τὴν Ἄμμωνος μαντείαν ἀγνοοῖ, πλέον τι οἰόμενος εἶναι λόγους γεγραμμένους τοῦ τὸν εἰδότα ὑπομνῆσαι περὶ ὧν ἂν ᾖ τὰ γεγραμμένα.

He would be an extremely simple person who thought written words do anything more than remind someone who knows about the matter of which they are written,

says Sokrates (275d). Technicians of reading and writing see in letters a means to fix thoughts and wisdom once and for all in usable and reusable form. Sokrates denies that wisdom can be fixed. When people read books they derive

... σοφίας δὲ τοῖς μαθηταῖς δόξαν, οὐκ ἀλήθειαν πορίζεις· πολυήκοοι γάρ σοι γενόμενοι ἄνευ διδαχῆς πολυγνώμονες εἶναι δόξουσιν, ἀγνώμονες ὡς ἐπὶ τὸ πλῆθος ὄντες, καὶ χαλεποὶ συνεῖναι, δοξόσοφοι γεγονότες ἀντὶ σοφῶν."

... the appearance of wisdom, not true wisdom, for they will read many things without instruction and will therefore seem to know many things, when they are for the most part ignorant and hard to get along with, since they are not wise, but only appear wise. (275b)

Sokrates conceives of wisdom as something alive, a "living breathing word" (*ton logon zōnta kai empsychon*, 276a), that happens between two people when they talk. Change is essential to it, not because wisdom changes but because people do, and must. In contrast, Sokrates emphasizes the peculiarly static nature of the written word:

Δεινὸν γάρ που, ὦ Φαῖδρε, τοῦτ᾽ ἔχει γραφή, καὶ ὡς ἀληθῶς ὅμοιον ζωγραφίᾳ. καὶ γὰρ τὰ ἐκείνης ἔκγονα ἕστηκε μὲν ὡς ζῶντα, ἐὰν δ᾽ ἀνέρῃ τι, σεμνῶς πάνυ σιγᾷ· ταὐτὸν δὲ καὶ οἱ λόγοι· δόξαις μὲν ἂν ὡς τι φρονοῦντας αὐτοὺς λέγειν, ἐὰν δέ τι ἔρῃ τῶν λεγομένων βουλόμενος μαθεῖν, ἕν τι σημαίνει μόνον ταὐτὸν ἀεί.

Writing, Phaedrus, has this strange power, quite like painting in fact; for the creatures in paintings stand there like living beings, yet if you ask them anything they maintain a solemn silence. It is the same with written words. You might imagine they speak as if they were actually thinking something but if you want to find out about what they are saying and question them, they keep on giving the one same message eternally. (275d-e)

Like painting, the written word fixes living things in time and space, giving them the appearance of animation although they are abstracted from life and incapable of change. *Logos* in its spoken form is a living, changing, unique process of thought. It happens once and is irrecoverable. The *logos* written down by a writer who knows his craft will approximate this living organism in the necessary ordering and interrelation of its parts:

ὥσπερ ζῷον συνεστάναι σῶμά τι ἔχοντα αὐτὸν αὐτοῦ, ὥστε μήτε ἀκέφαλον εἶναι μήτε ἄπουν, ἀλλὰ μέσα τε ἔχειν καὶ ἄκρα, πρέποντα ἀλλήλοις καὶ τῷ ὅλῳ γεγραμμένα.

organized like a live creature with a body of its own, not headless or footless but with middle and end fitted to one another and to the whole. (264c)

The *logos* of a bad writer, Lysias, for instance, does not even attempt this semblance of life, but throws words together in no order at all, perhaps beginning at the point where it should end and wholly ignorant of organic sequence. You can enter this *logos* at any point and find it saying the same thing. Once it is written down it continues to say that same thing forever over and over within itself, over and over in time. As communication, such a text is a dead letter.

Midas

Sokrates drives home his point about Lysias' bad writing with an analogy from the grave. "It is very like the inscription on the tomb of Midas the Phrygian," he says of Lysias' discourse, and proceeds to cite the inscription:

Χαλκῆ παρθένος εἰμί, Μίδα δ᾽ ἐπὶ σήματι κεῖμαι.
ὄφρ᾽ ἂν ὕδωρ τε νάῃ καὶ δένδρεα μακρὰ τεθήλῃ,
αὐτοῦ τῇδε μένουσα πολυκλαύτου ἐπὶ τύμβου,
ἀγγελέω παριοῦσι Μίδας ὅτι τῇδε τέθαπται.

Bronze maiden am I and on Midas' mound I lie.
As long as water flows and tall trees bloom,
Right here fixed fast on the tearful tomb,
I shall announce to all who pass near: Midas is dead
    and buried here!

The analogy is an artful one on several levels, for the inscription epitomizes in its form as well as in its content all that Sokrates says we should mistrust about the written word, and also aims specific satire at Lysias. The inscription is an epitaph: advertisement of death and a challenge to time. It promises to assert a single unchangeable fact in one unchanging form into eternity: Midas is dead. Its voice is that of a girl, youthful forever and proud to defy the world of time and change and living phenomena passing before her. With Midas, she holds aloof: he in death, she in letters.

Furthermore, Sokrates confides, this epitaph is distinctive in one feature of its composition. Every line is independent of every other, in sense and in meter, so that the poem yields much the same meaning in whatever order it is read:

ὅτι δ᾽ οὐδὲν διαφέρει αὐτοῦ πρῶτον ἢ ὕστατόν τι
λέγεσθαι, ἐννοεῖς που, ὡς ἐγῷμαι.

I suppose you notice (Sokrates says to Phaedrus) that it makes no difference which line is read first or which read last. (264e)

With this detail the inscription becomes specifically derisive of Lysias. It is fairly obvious how a poem whose lines are interchangeable may be compared with a speech that starts where it should end and follows no cogent order throughout its exposition. But let us train our attention, through this textual comparison, at the analogy in real life toward which it points. The Midas inscription has some salient details in common with the theory of love that Lysias expounds in his speech.

Like Lysias' nonlover, the words of the inscription stand aloof from time and declare their difference from the world of ephemeral beings. The nonlover bases his claim to moral superiority over the lover on this difference. He achieves his difference by sidestepping the moment which is 'now' for the man in love, that is, the moment of desire when the lover loses self-control. The nonlover, like the words on Midas' tomb, projects himself into the future. Standing outside the time of desire, he can stand also outside its emotions and regard all moments of the love affair as equal and interchangeable. Neither Lysias' erotic theory nor his speech acknowledges any necessary ordering of its parts in time. So, too, the words on Midas' tomb transcend the temporal order, in their form as in their content. Changeless themselves, they promise to the reader, as Lysias does to his beloved boy, unchanging consistency in the face of transforming time.

Now consider Midas himself. As a mythological symbol Midas deserves our passing consideration, for the statement made by his tomb repeats the central, disfiguring mistake of his life. It is a mistake from which the lover may have something to learn.

He is a paradoxical case, in the ancient view. Midas is used by Aristotle, for instance, to betoken the absurdity of want in the midst of wealth:

καίτοι ἄτοπον τοιοῦτον εἶναι πλοῦτον οὗ εὐπορῶν λιμῷ ἀπολεῖται, καθάπερ καὶ τὸν Μίδαν ἐκεῖνον μυθολογοῦσι διὰ τὴν ἀπληστίαν τῆς εὐχῆς πάντων αὐτῷ γιγνομένων τῶν παρατιθεμένων χρυσῶν.

It is an absurd thing [*atopon*] for wealth to be of such a kind that a man who is rich with it dies of starvation, like the mythological Midas: by reason of the insatiability of his prayer, everything set before him became gold. (*Pol.* 1.3.1257b)

Midas is an image of someone stranded in his own desire, longing to touch and not to touch at the same time, like the children in Sophokles' poem with their hands full of ice. Perfect desire is perfect impasse. What does the desirer want from desire? Candidly, he wants to keep on desiring.

Midas' golden touch would be a powerful symbol of perfect, self-extinguishing, self-perpetuating desire. As such, Midas might call to mind the type of bad lover whom Sokrates and Lysias denounce in their speeches, for Midas' touch has a devastating effect on the things he loves. They turn to gold. They stop in time. So, too, the bad lover contrives to fix the living organism of his *paidika* at a moment of gold, that is at the *akmē* of his youthful bloom, so that he may be perfectly enjoyable for as long as possible. The Midas touch stops time for the lover too, permitting him to freeze his own emotional life at the high point of desire.

Plato does not make explicit any connection between

Midas and the lover who wants to stop time; nonetheless, Midas may be selected for mention here partly in order to evoke the Midas touch as an image of desire. It is an important image because it helps to focus the central point at issue between Sokrates' and Lysias' theories of eros. Both theories agree that desire pulls the desirer into paradoxical relations with time. Both theories observe that the conventional *erastēs* responds to this problem with certain tactics, attempting to block the natural currents of physical and personal development that are moving his beloved through life. These tactics are damaging, Sokrates and Lysias concur; they do not concur at all on what tactics are preferable. Lysias recommends, through the fiction of his nonlover, that the best thing to do is simply stand aside from time. 'Now' is the moment that presents a problem, so imagine yourself at 'then' and avoid the problem. Sokrates refers to this tactic as "swimming backwards against the current" (264a) and likens it to the *jeu d'esprit* on Midas' tomb. But his objections are more than rhetorical, and he goes on to judge the Lysian attitude a crime against eros (242e). In the rest of the dialogue we come to see what this means: a Lysian theory of love violates those natural currents of physical and spiritual change that constitute our human situation in time. What happens when you choose to abstract yourself from participation in time? Plato gives us three different images of the answer.

Midas himself is one image. On his tomb, as in his life, Midas is surrounded by a world of changing phenomena in which he may not participate. His problems in life begin with insatiable greed and end in death by want, a paradox with significant cross-references for erotic desire. But his life and its implications remain an implicit feature of Plato's treatment, so perhaps we are not justified in drawing them out. We must turn to another category of creatures who appear in the dialogue, and who share Midas' dilemma in its main outlines as well as in its attitude to want.

Cicadas

Cicadas also spend their lives starving to death in pursuit of their desire. These insects enter the dialogue somewhat tangentially, as Sokrates is passing from one topic of conversation to another and notices them singing in the branches above. He points them out to Phaedrus:

... καὶ ἅμα μοι δοκοῦσιν ὡς ἐν τῷ πνίγει ὑπὲρ κεφαλῆς ἡμῶν οἱ τέττιγες ᾄδοντες καὶ ἀλλήλοις διαλεγόμενοι καθορᾶν καὶ ἡμᾶς.

... and the cicadas appear to be staring down at us, singing away in the heat over our heads and chatting with one another. . . . (258e)

Phaedrus is curious about cicadas so Sokrates goes on to supply some traditional lore:

λέγεται δ᾽ ὥς ποτ᾽ ἦσαν οὗτοι ἄνθρωποι τῶν πρὶν Μούσας γεγονέναι, γενομένων δὲ Μουσῶν καὶ φανείσης ᾠδῆς οὕτως ἄρα τινὲς τῶν τότε ἐξεπλάγησαν ὑφ᾽ ἡδονῆς, ὥστε ᾄδοντες ἠμέλησαν σίτων τε καὶ ποτῶν, καὶ ἔλαθον τελευτήσαντες αὑτούς· ἐξ ὧν τὸ τεττίγων γένος μετ᾽ ἐκεῖνο φύεται, γέρας τοῦτο παρὰ Μουσῶν λαβόν, μηδὲν τροφῆς δεῖσθαι γενόμενον, ἀλλ᾽ ἄσιτόν τε καὶ ἄποτον εὐθὺς ᾄδειν, ἕως ἂν τελευτήσῃ. . . .

Once upon a time, the story goes, cicadas were human beings, before the birth of the Muses. When the Muses were born and song came into being, some of these creatures were so struck by the pleasure of it that they sang and sang, forgot to eat and drink, and died before they knew it. From them the race of cicadas arose, and they have this special privilege from the Muses: from the time they are born they need no nourishment, they just sing continually without eating or drinking until they die.... (259b-c)

Like Midas, the cicadas can be read as an image of the fundamental erotic dilemma. They are creatures pulled into confrontation with time by their own desire. They enact a nobler version of this dilemma than Midas did, for their passion is musical, and they offer a new solution to the lover's paradox of 'now' and 'then.' The cicadas simply enter the 'now' of their desire and stay there. Abstracted from the processes of life, oblivious to time, they sustain the present indicative of pleasure from the instant they are born until, as Sokrates says, "they escape their own notice, having died" (*elathon teleutēsantes hautous*, 259c). Cicadas have no life apart from their desire and when it ends, so do they.

Here is an alternative to the tactics of Lysias' nonlover. The nonlover sidesteps painful transitions between 'now' and 'then' by stationing himself permanently at the end of desire. He sacrifices the intense and transient pleasure of the lover's 'now' in return for an extended 'then' of consistent emotion and predictable behavior. Cicadas choose the opposite sacrifice, investing their whole lives in the momentous delight of 'now.' Passing time and its transitions do not affect them. They are stranded in a living death of pleasure.

Unlike Midas, the cicadas are happy in their choice of life-as-death. Yet, they are cicadas. That is, they are creatures who were once men but who preferred to decline from human status because they found man's condition incompatible with their desire for pleasure. They are creatures whose sole activity in the course of a lifetime is the prosecution of that desire. It is not a choice open to human beings, nor to any organism that is committed to living in time. Organisms struck by desire, however, tend to misprize this commitment, as we have seen. Plato gives us one further image of what happens when they do so.

Gardening for Fun and Profit

It is an image of gardens (276b-77a). Lovers and writers and cicadas are not the only ones who find themselves at odds with time. Gardeners also have occasion to wish to evade, manipulate, and defy temporal conditions. The occasions are festive ones and, according to Sokrates, on such occasions gardeners become playful and gardening does not follow serious rules. Plato introduces the subject of gardens in order to make a point about the art of writing, whose seriousness he wishes to put into question. Let us consider first the play of gardening and then the play of writing. Plato brings them into erotic intersection in the so-called "gardens of Adonis."

The gardens of Adonis were a feature of Athenian religious observance in the fifth century. During annual rituals in honor of Adonis, seeds of wheat, barley, and fennel were sown in small pots and forced to grow unseasonably fast for enjoyment during the eight days of the festival. The plants had no roots. They bloomed briefly, withered almost at once, and were pitched out the day after the festival. Their hectic lives were meant to reflect that of Adonis himself, plucked in the bloom of his youth by the goddess Aphrodite, dead in his prime as a result (Diogenes Laertius 1.14; Gow 1952, 2:295). It is the fast and beautiful career of the ideal beloved.

Sokrates adduces these gardens of Adonis as an analogy for the written word, seductive and ephemeral as it is, a simulation of living discourse. In the midst of his appraisal of writing, he turns to Phaedrus with the question:

τόδε δή μοι εἰπέ· ὁ νοῦν ἔχων γεωργός, ὧν σπερμάτων
κήδοιτο καὶ ἔγκαρπα βούλοιτο γενέσθαι, πότερα
σπουδῇ ἂν θέρους εἰς Ἀδώνιδος κήπους ἀρῶν χαίροι
θεωρῶν καλοὺς ἐν ἡμέραισιν ὀκτὼ γιγνομένους, ἢ
ταῦτα μὲν δὴ παιδιᾶς τε καὶ ἑορτῆς χάριν δρῴη ἄν,
ὅτε καὶ ποιοῖ· ἐφ᾽ οἷς δὲ ἐσπούδακεν, τῇ γεωργικῇ
χρώμενος ἂν τέχνῃ, σπείρας εἰς τὸ προσῆκον, ἀγαπῴη
ἂν ἐν ὀγδόῳ μηνὶ ὅσα ἔσπειρεν τέλος λαβόντα;

Now tell me this. Do you think a sensible gardener,
who cared for his seeds and wished to see them bear
fruit, would plant them with serious intention in
gardens of Adonis at high summer and take pleasure
in watching them grow beautiful in a space of eight
days? Or would he do that sort of thing, when he did
it at all, only for fun or a festival? And, when he was
serious, would he not apply his skill as a gardener
and sow in fitting soil and be gratified when the
seeds he had sown came to full bloom in the eighth
month?   (276b)

No gardener serious about growing plants would in-
dulge in the hasty, cosmetic agriculture of the gardens of
Adonis, Sokrates and Phaedrus proceed to agree. By the
same token, no thinker serious about communicating
thoughts would choose to "sow them in ink with a reed-
pen" (276c). Gardens of letters, like gardens of Adonis,
are sown for fun (276d). Serious thoughts need different
cultivation and time to grow; planted as seeds of living
speech in the ground of an appropriate soul, they will
take root, ripen, and bear fruit as knowledge in due sea-
son (276e-277a). At this point in the dialogue Sokrates
lays his belief candidly and emphatically before Phaedrus: serious thoughts and knowledge have their real life
in philosophical conversation, not in the games of reading and writing.

Like his analogy from the tomb of Midas, Plato's analogy from gardens tells specifically against the *logos* of

Lysias with its peculiarly inorganic style of rhetoric, and generally against the cultivation of letters as a substitute for dialectic. The gardens draw our attention, even more pointedly than Midas' inscription, to the factor of time that is at the core of Plato's worry about reading and writing. Written texts make available the notion that one *knows* what one has merely *read*. For Plato this notion is a dangerous delusion; he believes the reach for knowledge to be a process that is necessarily lived out in space and time. Attempts to shortcut the process, or package it for convenient reuse, as in the form of a written treatise, are a denial of our commitment to time and cannot be taken seriously. Plants that bloom for eight days with no roots are an image of this quick-access *sophia*. At the same time, the urgent agriculture of Adonis reminds us of Lysias' erotic *logos*, which starts where it should end and achieves its rhetorical and conceptual purposes by a violent shortcut through the beginning stages of love. In their wish to control time, then, writers and gardeners intersect in Plato's analogy. But let us look closer at the analogy. There is a third angle here and, as with the myth of Midas, it unfolds in an image of the damage that lovers can do to those they love.

Consider the plants of Adonis, forced too quickly to their *akmē*, held at the peak of their bloom while the festival lasts, discarded the next day: this is an image of how the conventional *erastēs* uses his *paidika*. It is an image of one human being exploiting another by controlling the time of his life.

ἔτι τοίνυν ἄγαμον, ἄπαιδα, ἄοικον ὅτι πλεῖστον χρόνον παιδικὰ ἐραστὴς εὔξαιτ᾽ ἂν γενέσθαι, τὸ αὐτοῦ γλυκὺ ὡς πλεῖστον χρόνον καρποῦσθαι ἐπιθυμῶν.

The lover will passionately wish his *paidika* to remain unmarried and childless and homeless for as long a time as possible, since it is his desire to reap the fruit of what is sweet to himself for as long a time as possible.　(240a)

So Sokrates describes the manipulative tendencies of the conventional *erastēs*. This lover prefers to play his erotic games with a partner who has neither roots nor future.

Something Serious

Is Missing

The static blooms of Adonis provide us with an answer
to our question 'What would the lover ask of time?' As
Plato formulates it, the answer brings us once again to
the perception that lovers and readers have very similar
desires. And the desire of each is something paradoxical.
As lover you want ice to *be* ice and yet not melt in your
hands. As reader you want knowledge to *be* knowledge
and yet lie fixed on a written page. Such wants cannot
help but pain you, at least in part, because they place you
at a blind point from which you watch the object of your
desire disappear into itself.

Plato is perfectly aware of that pain. He re-creates it
over and over again in his dialectic, and its experience is
intrinsic to the kind of understanding he wishes to communicate. In the *Phaedrus* we have observed this re-cre-
ation especially on the analogic level. Plato's analogies
are not flat diagrams in which one image (for example,
gardens) is superimposed on another (the written word)
in exact correspondence. An analogy is constructed in
three-dimensional space. Its images float one upon the
other without convergence: there is something in between, something paradoxical: Eros.

Eros is the unspoken ground of all that happens between Adonis and Aphrodite in myth, which is reenacted
in the ritual of gardens. Eros is the ground where *logos*
takes root between two people who are having a conversation, which may be reenacted on the written page. Rit-

uals and reenactments take place outside the real time of people's lives, in a suspended moment of control. We love such suspended time for the sake of its difference from ordinary time and real life. We love the activities that are placed within suspended time, like festivals and reading, for their essential unseriousness. This love worries Plato. A person seduced by it may think to replace real time with the kind of time appropriate only in rituals or in books. That would be a serious, damaging mistake, in Plato's view. For, as there is no exact correspondence between rootless plants and a dying Adonis, so there is only a symbolic correspondence between written words and real *logos*. The person who mistakes symbol for reality is left with a dead garden, or with a love affair such as Lysias prescribes for the nonlover. Something is missing from such a love affair, as life is missing from the garden, something essential: Eros.

Takeover

He had the same attitude to his life as a sculptor to his statue or a novelist to his novel. One of a novelist's inalienable rights is to be able to rework his novel. If he takes a dislike to the beginning, he can rewrite it or cross it out entirely. But Zdena's existence deprived Mirek of his prerogative as an author. Zdena insisted on remaining part of the opening pages of the novel. She refused to be crossed out.

Milan Kundera, *The Book of*
Laughter and Forgetting

Plato presents Lysias as someone who thinks himself able to control all the risks, alarms and inebriations of eros by means of a prodigious emotional calculus. The Lysian strategy of life and love applies to real erotic events a set of tactics that are by now familiar to us. The Lysian nonlover steps aside from the moving current of his beloved's life and places himself at a point of aesthetic distance. It is the vantage point of the writer. Lysias' insights on eros are a writer's insights, and the theory of control he expounds treats the experience of love as a fixed text that can be begun anywhere or read backwards and render the same sense. It is a bad speech, and the nonlover would make a tedious *erastēs*. Yet the speech at one time seduced Phaedrus. He read it over and over as if in love with the words (228b; cf. 236b). There is a terrible power in the Lysian *logos*. What is it?

Lysias' text offers to its readers something that no one who has been in love could fail to covet: self-control.

How do apparently external events enter and take control of one's psyche? This question, especially in its erotic versions, obsessed the Greeks. We have seen how Homer framed the question in his *Iliad*, as an encounter between Helen and Aphrodite on the wall of Troy (3.400ff). Aphrodite materializes out of nowhere, in the midst of an otherwise ordinary afternoon, and enjoins desire upon Helen. There is a flurry of resistance on Helen's part; Aphrodite flattens it with a single threat. Desire is a moment with no way out. Consistently throughout the Greek lyric corpus, as well as in the poetry of tragedy and comedy, eros is an experience that assaults the lover from without and proceeds to take control of his body, his mind and the quality of his life. Eros comes out of nowhere, on wings, to invest the lover, to deprive his body of vital organs and material substance, to enfeeble his mind and distort its thinking, to replace normal conditions of health and sanity with disease and madness. The poets represent eros as an invasion, an illness, an insanity, a wild animal, a natural disaster. His action is to melt, break down, bite into, burn, devour, wear away, whirl around, sting, pierce, wound, poison, suffocate, drag off or grind the lover to a powder. Eros employs nets, arrows, fire, hammers, hurricanes, fevers, boxing gloves or bits and bridles in making his assault. No one can fight Eros off (*Homeric Hymn to Hermes* 434; Sappho, *LP*, fr. 130.2; Soph. *Ant.* 781; *Trach.* 441; Eur., *TGF*, fr. 433; cf. Pl. *Symp.* 196d). Very few see him coming. He lights on you from somewhere outside yourself and, as soon as he does, you are taken over, changed radically. You cannot resist the change or control it or come to terms with it. It is in general a change for the worse, at best a mixed blessing (*glukupikron*, as Sappho says). That is the poets' standard attitude and conviction.

Addressing a fifth-century audience educated in the poets, Plato is writing for men imbued with this conviction. Lysias himself bespeaks the poetic tradition, for his

determinative assumption in showing how damaging
eros can be is that the conventional *erastēs* is someone
out of his own control:

> καὶ γὰρ αὐτοὶ ὁμολογοῦσι νοσεῖν μᾶλλον ἢ σωφρο-
> νεῖν, καὶ εἰδέναι ὅτι κακῶς φρονοῦσιν, ἀλλ᾽ οὐ δύ-
> νασθαι αὐτῶν κρατεῖν·

For indeed lovers themselves admit that they are sick
not sane, and know they are not in their right minds,
but they are not able to control themselves. (231d)

The lover mastered by eros cannot answer for his own
mind or actions. From this condition, which the Greeks
call erotic madness or *mania*, the lover's harmfulness
ensues.

As soon as eros enters his life, the lover is lost, for he
goes mad. But where is the point of entry? When does desire begin? That is a very difficult moment to find, until it
is too late. When you are falling in love it is always already too late: *dēute*, as the poets say. To be able to iso-
late the moment when love begins, and so block its entry
or avoid it entirely, would put you in control of eros. Lysias' nonlover claims to have achieved such control. He
does not say how and the claim remains psychologically
incredible. His *logos* simply ignores the moment when
eros begins; he speaks from the end of the love affair as
one who has never been taken over by desire at all. Nonlovers are people who remain "masters of themselves"
(232a).

Sokrates denies that such control is ever possible, or
even desirable, for human beings. He speaks of it as an
economy of death:

> ... ἡ δὲ ἀπὸ τοῦ μὴ ἐρῶντος οἰκειότης, σωφροσύνῃ
> θνητῇ κεκραμένη, θνητά τε καὶ φειδωλὰ οἰκονομοῦσα,
> ἀνελευθερίαν ὑπὸ πλήθους ἐπαινουμένην ὡς ἀρε-
> τὴν τῇ φίλῃ ψυχῇ ἐντεκοῦσα. ...

... the intimacy of the nonlover is mixed with a mortal self-control [*sōphrosynē thnētē*] which disburses itself in mortal miserly measurings [*thnēta te kai pheidōla oikonomousa*] and engenders in the beloved soul that spirit of begrudgement commonly praised as virtue. ... (256e)

It is a deadly stinginess by which the nonlover eludes desire. He measures his emotions out like a miser counting gold. There is no risk entailed in his transaction with eros because he does not invest in the single moment that is open to risk, the moment when desire begins, 'now.' 'Now' is the moment when change erupts. The nonlover declines change, as successfully as the cicadas do, enclosed in a carapace of *sōphrosynē*. He is secure in his narrative choices of life and love. He already knows how the novel will end, and he has firmly crossed out the beginning.

Read Me the Bit Again

> Read me the bit
> again about the thing
> that is pure. . . .
> read that bit, the thing
> we cannot turn our eyes to,
> you begin it.
>
> John Holloway, "Cone"

But Sokrates keeps insisting on the beginning. After Phaedrus has read Lysias' speech to him once through, he asks him to reread the opening words:

Ἴθι δή μοι ἀνάγνωθι τὴν τοῦ Λυσίου λόγου ἀρχήν.

Come on, read me the beginning of Lysias' speech.
. . . (262d)

And then he asks him to reread it again:

βούλει πάλιν ἀναγνῶμεν τὴν ἀρχὴν αὐτοῦ;

Please, will you reread his beginning one more time? (263e)

Phaedrus is politely reluctant. He knows there is no beginning to be found in it, and he says so:

Εἰ σοί γε δοκεῖ· ὃ μέντοι ζητεῖς οὐκ ἔστ᾽ αὐτόθι.

Yes, I will if you like, but the thing
you are looking for is not there. (263e)

The thing Sokrates is looking for is the 'now' of desire. But Lysias' first sentence already puts the erotic relation-

ship in the past tense. The nonlover starts off by saying
to his boy:

Περὶ μὲν τῶν ἐμῶν πραγμάτων ἐπίστασαι, καὶ ὡς
νομίζω συμφέρειν ἡμῖν γενομένων τούτων ἀκήκοας·

My business you know and, as to how I think these
things that have transpired between us should turn
out, you have heard. (230e7 = 262e2 = 263e7)

The fact that Sokrates cannot find the beginning of
Lysias' *logos*, or of Lysias' eros, is crucial. Beginnings are
crucial. Sokrates emphasizes in the most dignified language (245c-46) that everything in existence has a beginning, with one exception: the beginning itself. Only the
archē itself controls its own beginning. It is this very control that Lysias usurps when he takes his pen and crosses
out the beginning of eros for his nonlover. But this act is
fiction. In reality the beginning is the one moment that
you, as an unwitting target of winged Eros, cannot control. All that this moment brings, both good and evil, bitter and sweet, comes gratuitously and unpredictably—a
gift of the gods, as the poets say. From that moment on,
the story is largely up to you, but the beginning is not. In
this realization lies the critical difference between Sokrates' and Lysias' erotic thinking. Sokrates has Phaedrus search Lysias' *logos* for a beginning, in vain, to
make a point. The beginning is not fictive. It cannot be
placed in the control of a writer or reader. We should
note that the Greek verb 'to read' is *anagignōskein*, a
compound of the verb 'to know' (*gignōskein*) and the
prefix *ana*, meaning 'again.' If you are reading, you are
not at the beginning.

As Sokrates tells it, your story begins the moment Eros
enters you. That incursion is the biggest risk of your life.
How you handle it is an index of the quality, wisdom and
decorum of the things inside you. As you handle it you
come into contact with what is inside you, in a sudden

and startling way. You perceive what you are, what you lack, what you could be. What is this mode of perception, so different from ordinary perception that it is well described as madness? How is it that when you fall in love you feel as if suddenly you are seeing the world as it really is? A mood of knowledge floats out over your life. You seem to know what is real and what is not. Something is lifting you toward an understanding so complete and clear it makes you jubilant. This mood is no delusion, in Sokrates' belief. It is a glance down into time, at realities you once knew, as staggeringly beautiful as the glance of your beloved (249e-50c).

The point of time that Lysias deletes from his *logos*, the moment of *mania* when Eros enters the lover, is for Sokrates the single most important moment to confront and grasp. 'Now' is a gift of the gods and an access onto reality. To address yourself to the moment when Eros glances into your life and to grasp what is happening in your soul at that moment is to begin to understand how to live. Eros' mode of takeover is an education: it can teach you the real nature of what is inside you. Once you glimpse that, you can begin to become it. Sokrates says it is a glimpse of a god (253a).

Sokrates' answer to the erotic dilemma of time, then, is the antithesis of Lysias' answer. Lysias chooses to edit out 'now' and narrate entirely from the vantage point of 'then.' In Sokrates' view, to cross out 'now' is, in the first place, impossible, a writer's impertinence. Even if it were possible, it would mean losing a moment of unique and indispensable value. Sokrates proposes instead to assimilate 'now' in such a way that it prolongs itself over the whole of life, and beyond. Sokrates would inscribe his novel within the instant of desire. We should begin to keep an eye on this Sokratic literary ambition, because it will have a serious effect on the story Plato is telling in the *Phaedrus*. It will make it disappear.

Then Ends Where Now Begins

On the observable facts of erotic experience Sokrates and Lysias are in rough agreement, but there is a world of difference between the readings they give to those facts. The facts are that eros changes you so drastically you seem to become a different person. In conventional thinking, such changes are best categorized as madness. What is the best thing to do with a mad person? Write him out of your novel, is Lysias' answer. It is an answer that would make some sense to his contemporaries, for his version of eros proceeds from thoroughly conventional premises. It conceives of desire, in the terms of a longstanding poetic tradition, as devastating takeover of the self and a generally negative experience. It assumes, as was standard in the popular moral thinking of the day, self-control or *sōphrosynē* as the rule of an enlightened life. Sokrates subverts both clichés. His approach is radical. He does not doubt that a nonlover will rise to feats of *sōphrosynē*. He does not deny that eros is takeover, a form of *mania*, but he vindicates *mania*. Let us see how.

Change of self is loss of self, according to the traditional Greek attitude. Categorized as madness, it is held to be an unquestionable evil. Sokrates does not agree:

λεκτέος δὲ ὧδε, ὅτι Οὐκ ἔστ᾽ ἔτυμος λόγος ὃς ἂν παρόντος ἐραστοῦ τῷ μὴ ἐρῶντι μᾶλλον φῇ δεῖν χαρίζεσθαι, διότι δὴ ὁ μὲν μαίνεται, ὁ δὲ σωφρονεῖ. εἰ μὲν γὰρ ἦν ἁπλοῦν τὸ μανίαν κακὸν εἶναι, καλῶς ἂν ἐλέγετο· νῦν δὲ τὰ μέγιστα τῶν ἀγαθῶν ἡμῖν γίγνεται διὰ μανίας, θείᾳ μέντοι δόσει διδομένης.

I must say this story [*logos*] is not true, the story that a nonlover should be gratified in preference to a lover on the grounds that the latter is mad while the former is sane. Now, if it were a simple fact that madness [*mania*] is evil, the story would be fine. But the fact is, the greatest of good things come to us through madness when it is conferred as a gift of the gods. (244a)

Sokrates' central argument, as he goes on to reevaluate madness, is that you keep your mind to yourself at the cost of closing out the gods. Truly good and indeed divine things are alive and active outside you and should be let in to work their changes. Such incursions formally instruct and enrich our lives in society; no prophet or healer or poet could practice his art if he did not lose his mind, Sokrates says (244a-45). Madness is the instrument of such intelligence. More to the point, erotic *mania* is a valuable thing in private life. It puts wings on your soul.

Sokrates' exposition of *mania* as a profitable experience for the individual depends on a theory of the dynamics of the soul that is carefully crafted to respond to the questions of erotic control raised by traditional poetry. His analysis subsumes, and at the same time subverts, the poets' standard metaphors of eros so that he may recast their traditional picture of erotic experience. Where they see loss and damage, Sokrates insists on profit and growth. Where they see ice melting, he says wings grow. Where they brace themselves against takeover, he unfolds himself for flight.

Despite elementary points of concurrence, there is an enormous difference, in the end, between the erotic attitudes of Sokrates, on the one hand, Lysias and traditional Greek sentiment on the other. It is a fine thing to see Plato sum up all that difference in one image. Wings, in traditional poetry, are the mechanism by which Eros swoops upon the unsuspecting lover to wrest control of his person and personality. Wings are an instrument of damage and a symbol of irresistible power. When you fall in love, change sweeps through you on wings and you cannot help but lose your grip on that cherished entity, your self. We have seen how Sappho describes the loss of self in fragment 31. As desire takes over her body, mind and perceptual functions she says *eptoaisen*, which means something like "it puts the heart in my chest on wings" or "it makes my heart fly inside me" (31.6). Anakreon speaks of the same sensation, and assigns to it the same cause:

ἀναπέτομαι δὴ πρὸς Ὄλυμπον πτερύγεσσι κούφῃς
διὰ τὸν Ἔρωτ᾽· οὐ γὰρ ἐμοὶ ⟨‒ ⏑⟩ θέλει συνηβᾶν.

I am soaring toward Olympos on light wings
for the sake of Eros, for [the boy I desire] is not
willing to share his youth with me.
(378 *PMG*)

The desire that drove Helen mad is represented by Alkaios in similar terms:

κὰλένας ἐν στήθ[ε]σιν [ἐ]πτ[όαις
θῦμον Ἀργείας Τρὼω δ[.].αν[
ἐκμάνεισα ξ[ε.]ναπάτα πιπ[
ἔσπετο νᾶϊ

... [Eros] made Helen's heart fly like a wing in her
chest
and she went out of her mind for a Trojan man
and followed him over the sea. . . .
(*LP*, fr. 283.3-6)

The significance of Eros' wings has become a poetic *topos* by Hellenistic times, as we see in this epigram of Archias:

"Φεύγειν δεῖ τὸν Ἔρωτα" κενὸς πόνος· οὐ γὰρ ἀλύξω
πεζὸς ὑπὸ πτηνοῦ πυκνὰ διωκόμενος.

"You should flee Eros": empty effort!
How shall I elude on foot one who chases me on
wings?

(*Anth. Pal. 5.59*)

Plato takes the traditional wings of Eros and reimagines them. Wings are no foreign machinery of invasion in Plato's conception. They have natural roots in each soul, a residue of its immortal beginnings. Our souls once lived on wings among the gods, he says, nourished as gods are by the infinite elation of looking at reality all the time. Now we are exiled from that place and quality of life, yet we remember it from time to time, for example, when we look upon beauty and fall in love (246-51). Moreover, we have the power to recover it, by means of the soul's wings. Sokrates describes how the wings will grow, given the right conditions, powerful enough to carry the soul back to its beginnings. When you fall in love you feel all sorts of sensations inside you, painful and pleasant at once: it is your wings sprouting (251-52). It is the beginning of what you mean to be.

Beginnings are crucial. It becomes clearer now why Sokrates is so intent on them. For Sokrates, the moment when eros begins is a glimpse of the immortal 'beginning' that is a soul. The 'now' of desire is a shaft sunk into time and emerging onto timelessness, where the gods float, rejoicing in reality (247d-e). When you enter 'now,' you remember what it is like to be really alive, as gods are. There is something paradoxical in this 'memory' of a time that is timeless. The real difference between Sokrates' and Lysias' erotic theories resides in this paradox. Lysias is appalled by the paradox of desire and crosses it out: for him every erotic 'now' is the beginning of an end, and no more. He prefers a changeless, unending 'then.' But Sokrates looks at the paradoxical moment called 'now' and notices a curious movement taking place there. At the point where the soul begins itself, a blind point seems to open out. Into the blind point 'then' disappears.

What a Difference
a Wing Makes

A god can do it. But will you tell me how
a man can penetrate through the lyre's strings?
Our mind is split.

Rilke, *The Sonnets to Orpheus*

Wings mark the difference between a mortal and an immortal story of love. Lysias abhors the beginning of eros because he thinks it is really an end; Sokrates rejoices in the beginning in his belief that, really, it can have no end. So too, the presence or absence of wings in a lover's story determines his erotic strategy. That miserly and mortal *sōphrosynē* (256e) by which Lysias measures out his erotic experience is a tactic of defense against the change of self that eros imposes. Change is risk. What makes the risk worthwhile?

On the negative side, the *Phaedrus* gives us several images of changelessness. We have seen how, in their various ways, Midas and the cicadas and the garden of Adonis stand unalterably aloof from the processes of a life in time. The images are not encouraging: at best you will "escape your own notice having died" (cf. 259c). More positively, Sokrates' myth of wings is a glimpse of what mortals stand to gain from the entry of eros into their lives. But we should look very closely at this glimpse and the way in which Sokrates unfolds it. He is not at all naive about the terms of the transaction involved. Falling in love gives you access to an infinite good. But it is also very clear that, when Eros impinges on you in his true form, something is lost, something hard to measure. When you fall in love you abandon the forms of ordinary life. The lover's only care is to be with his beloved. All else slips into insignificance, as Sokrates describes:

> . . . ἀλλὰ μητέρων τε καὶ ἀδελφῶν καὶ ἑταίρων πάντων λέλησται, καὶ οὐσίας δι᾽ ἀμέλειαν ἀπολλυμένης παρ᾽ οὐδὲν τίθεται, νομίμων δὲ καὶ εὐσχημόνων, οἷς πρὸ τοῦ ἐκαλλωπίζετο, πάντων καταφρονήσασα δουλεύειν ἑτοίμη καὶ κοιμᾶσθαι ὅπου ἂν ἐᾷ τις ἐγγυτάτω τοῦ πόθου·

> . . . he forgets his mother and his brothers and all his comrades, couldn't care less if his property is lost through neglect, and, in disdain of all those proprieties and decorums whose beauty he once cherished, he is ready to be a slave, to sleep anywhere he is allowed, as close as possible to his desire.   (252a)

Falling in love, it seems, dislocates your view of what is significant. Aberrant behavior ensues. Rules of decorum go by the wayside. This is the common experience (*pathos*) of lovers, Sokrates says, to which men give the name Eros (252b).

But Eros has another name, Sokrates suddenly announces, and proceeds to develop this curious revelation into a pun. Inasmuch as puns are a somewhat preposterous form of reasoning and verge on injustice in their persuasive power, serious authors feel obliged to apologize when they use them, so Sokrates cautions Phaedrus that his pun is "pretty outrageous" (*hybristikon panu*, 252a) and perhaps untrue ("you can credit this or not," he concludes, 252c). Besides, it is unmetrical. For the pun is contained in two spurious lines of Homer, and the second line does not scan. The lines address themselves to the difference between the language spoken by gods and that of men. As far as the word for desire is concerned, the difference is a matter of only two letters:

τὸν δ᾽ ἤτοι θνητοὶ μὲν Ἔρωτα καλοῦσι ποτηνόν,
ἀθάνατοι δὲ Πτέρωτα, διὰ πτεροφύτορ᾽ ἀνάγκην.

Now mortals call him winged Eros
but immortals call him Pteros, because of the wing-
growing necessity.

(252c)

By adding *pt-* to Eros, the gods create Pteros, which is a
play upon the Greek word *pteron* meaning 'wing.' In the
language of gods, then, desire itself is known as 'the
winged one' or 'he who has something to do with wings.'
Why? The gods have a reason for their Pteros, namely
that desire entails a "wing-growing necessity."
It is an old idea in Greek that the gods have their own
language. Homer alludes to the divine language several
times (*Il.* 1.403-404; 2.813; 14.290-91; 20.74; *Od.*
10.305; 12.61) and Plato takes up the matter in his *Cratylus* (391ff). Modern philologists are of the opinion that
we have here a vestige of the difference between Greek
and pre-Greek populations of the mainland. The ancients took a bolder view. "Clearly the gods call things by
the names which are naturally right," says Sokrates in the
Cratylus (391e). It would be nice to believe that divine
names have a clearer meaning or a larger significance
than mortal ones. Unfortunately, one cannot easily see
this in most of the extant examples, but it was apparently
a viable opinion in Plato's day and is certainly part of
Sokrates' implication in the *Phaedrus*, as well as in the
Cratylus. "Surely gods call themselves by their true
names," is his assertion in the *Cratylus* (400e). Pteros is
truer than Eros.

Pteros can be said to have more truth than Eros because it tells us not just what desire should be named, but
why. Or, as Sokrates puts it, the gods' name includes
both the *pathos* (describable experience) and the *aitia*
(definitive cause or reason) of desire (252c). It is apparent
from the first line of the Homeric quotation that mortals,
even in their ignorance of his true name, were perceptive

enough to call Eros 'winged'—that is, they had grasped the *pathos* of the experience, had felt desire swoop through their insides. But they had no notion why this experience should have this particular character. They had not grasped the *aitia* of the feeling. Gods know the reason why things are, necessarily, the way they are. Out of this knowledge they name their names.

Pteros, then, represents a net gain on the semantic level. But as poetry it blunders. Sokrates warns us that his quotation is unmetrical; he leaves it to us to perceive that Pteros itself is the word responsible for dislocating the rhythm of the second line. Here is the problem: the verse is a dactylic hexameter and scans fine except for the word *de*, which precedes the divine name Pteros. *De* is by nature a single short syllable and stands at a position in the line that requires a short syllable; the rules of Greek prosody, however, regularly call for a short syllable, when it is followed by two consonants, to become a long syllable. Thus the *pt*- with which the gods enlarge *erōs* forces this verse into a metrical dilemma. It is a dilemma with a familiar contour: we might be reminded of the children in Sophokles' poem who want to hold ice in their hands and also want to put it down. *De* cannot be both a long syllable and a short syllable at the same time, at least not in reality as we see it.

Gods evidently see reality differently. But it is not surprising if their better version of the truth resists reduction to human measures. They are, after all, infinite beings and ancient thought is imbued with the notion of an incommensurability between their ways and ours. Plato gives this cliché a particular, meaningful turn in his Homeric quotation. Pteros disrupts our metrics in just the way that Eros deforms our lives. Meter, essentially, is an attempt to control words in time. We impose such control in the interests of beauty. But when Eros flashes into your life he brings his own standard of beauty and simply cancels out "all those proprieties and decorums whose beauty you once cherished" (252a).

Plato's bit of botched epic verse epitomizes our human transaction with Eros. Its terms are wrenching. We may profit enlargement of meaning, by admitting Eros in his true godly form as Pteros, but only at the cost of the formal beauty of our line of verse. Reversing these terms we see a reflection of Lysias who, with the craft and calculation of a novelist, designs a formally perfect love affair that has no meaning at all.

Eros' wings mark a critical difference between gods and men, for they defy human expression. Our words are too small, our rhythms too restrictive. But the true meaning of desire eludes our mortal grasp not only on the level of orthographic and metrical convention, that is, not only on the level of form. Even when we glimpse Eros in his divine version, even when a line of poetry gives us accidental access to the true *pathos* and *aitia* of desire, we do not necessarily catch on. For example, what does the poet of these two epic lines intend by the phrase "wing-growing necessity"? The translation is inept because the translator does not know what it means. This phrase ostensibly supplies us with a divine *aitia* for the true name of Eros. But whose are the wings and whose is the necessity? Does Eros have wings? Does Eros need wings? Does Eros cause others to have or to need wings? Does Eros need to cause others to have wings? Does Eros need to cause others to need to have wings? Various possibilities, not incompatible with one another, float out from the epic quotation. It is arguable that in their enhancing way the gods mean to imply all the possibilities at once when they use the name Pteros. But we cannot know that. As Sokrates says to his interlocutor in the *Cratylus*, when they are discussing this very question of divine names and their truth-value: "No doubt these are larger matters than you or I can figure out" (382b).

For a modern reader, prospects of figuring out the truth about Eros' name are even bleaker than they were for Sokrates or for Plato or for Plato's audience. We (modern readers) are the victims of a dubious textual tradition at this point in the *Phaedrus*. The manuscripts transmit three different readings of the adjective here rendered as "wing-growing." Since the adjective is likely a Platonic invention, problems of transmission are not surprising, or insurmountable: *'pterophutor'* ('wing-growing') emerges clearly as the most plausible reading. Yet our doubts about the text serve to confirm and sharpen Plato's point, in a way he could not have predicted but might truly have appreciated. No matter what technologies we devise, the knowledge of Eros available to us is no clear or certain thing (cf. *Phdr.* 275c). Gods may know exactly what is meant by the name Pteros or by a phrase like "wing-growing necessity" but, in the end, we do not. We do our utmost to grasp the *pathos* of erotic experience as it soars through our lives, but the *aitia* folds itself away and disappears into the written words of Plato's text.

What Is This Dialogue About?

old pond
frog jumps in
plop

Basho

The *Phaedrus* is an exploration of the dynamics and dangers of controlled time that make themselves accessible to readers, writers, and lovers. In Sokrates' view, a true *logos* has this in common with a real love affair, that it must be lived out in time. It is not the same backwards as forwards, it cannot be entered at any point, or frozen at its acme, or dismissed when fascination falters. A reader, like a bad lover, may feel he can zoom into his text at any point and pluck the fruit of its wisdom. A writer, like Lysias, may feel he can rearrange the limbs of the fiction on which he dotes with no regard for its life as an organism in time. So readers and writers dabble in the glamor of *grammata* without submitting themselves to wholesale erotic takeover or the change of self entailed in it. Like Odysseus bound to the mast of his ship, a reader may titillate himself with the siren song of knowledge and sail past intact. It is a kind of voyeurism, as we see when we watch Phaedrus seduced by the written words of Lysias. In Plato's view, the Lysian text is as philosophic pornography when compared with the erotic *logos* of Sokrates. But Plato cannot demonstrate this merely by aligning Lysias and Sokrates as one dead text beside another. The demonstration requires something of a ruse if it is to be truly arresting.

So Plato floats *logos* upon *logos*; they neither converge nor cancel out. We have seen other writers contrive such stereoscopic images. For example, Sappho in her fragment 31 superimposes one level of desire upon another, floats the actual upon the possible, in such a way that our perception jumps from one to the other without losing sight of the difference between them. Or again, the novelist Longus floats an apple upon a tree plucked bare of fruit, defying logic and captivating Daphnis. Or consider Zeno who, in his famous paradoxes, suspends moving objects upon the impossibility of motion, so that we see Achilles running as fast as he can, going nowhere. These are writers who share a strategy; they purpose to re-create in you a certain action of the mind and heart—the action of reaching out toward a meaning not yet known. It is a reach that never quite arrives, bittersweet. Plato's interplay of *logoi* in the *Phaedrus* imitates this reaching action. As Phaedrus reads what Lysias wrote, as Phaedrus listens to what Sokrates says, something begins to come into focus. You begin to understand what a *logos* is and what it is not and the difference between them. Eros is the difference. Like a face crossing a mirror at the back of the room, Eros moves. You reach. Eros is gone.

The *Phaedrus* is a written dialogue that ends by discrediting written dialogues. This fact does not cease to charm its readers. Indeed, it is the fundamental erotic feature of this *erōtikos logos*. Each time you read it, you are conducted to a place where something paradoxical happens: the knowledge of Eros that Sokrates and Phaedrus have been unfolding word by word through the written text simply steps into a blind point and vanishes, pulling the *logos* in after it. Their conversation about love (227a-57c) turns into a conversation about writing (257c-79c) and Eros is not seen or heard from again. This act of dialectical interception has, since antiquity, perplexed those who wish to say concisely what the dialogue is about. But there is nothing inappropriate here. If you reach into the *Phaedrus* to get hold of Eros, you will be eluded, necessarily. He never looks at you from the place from which you see him. Something moves in the space between. That is the most erotic thing about Eros.

Mythoplokos

Affection! thy intention stabs the centre
Thou dost make possible things not so held,
Communicat'st with dreams;—how can this be?—
With what's unreal thou coactive art,
And fellow'st nothing.

Shakespeare, *The Winter's Tale*

Imagine a city where there is no desire. Supposing for the
moment that the inhabitants of the city continue to eat,
drink and procreate in some mechanical way; still, their
life looks flat. They do not theorize or spin tops or speak
figuratively. Few think to shun pain; none give gifts.
They bury their dead and forget where. Zeno finds himself elected mayor and is set to work copying the legal
code on sheets of bronze. Now and again a man and a
woman may marry and live very happily, as travellers
who meet by chance at an inn; at night falling asleep they
dream the same dream, where they watch fire move
along a rope that binds them together, but it is unlikely
they remember the dream in the morning. The art of storytelling is widely neglected.
  A city without desire is, in sum, a city of no imagination. Here people think only what they already know.
Fiction is simply falsification. Delight is beside the point
(a concept to be understood in historical terms). This city
has an akinetic soul, a condition that Aristotle might explain in the following way. Whenever any creature is
moved to reach out for what it desires, Aristotle says,
that movement begins in an act of the imagination,

which he calls *phantasia*. Without such acts neither animals nor men would bestir themselves to reach out of the present condition or beyond what they already know. *Phantasia* stirs minds to movement by its power of representation; in other words, imagination prepares desire by representing the desired object as desirable to the mind of the desirer. *Phantasia* tells the mind a story. The story must make one thing clear, namely, the difference between what is present/actual/known and what is not, the difference between the desirer and the desired (Arist., *De An.* 3.10.433a-b).

We have seen what shape this story takes when poets tell it in lyric poems, when novelists write it into novels, when philosophers construe it as dialectic. In order to communicate the difference between what is present/actual/known and what is lacking/possible/unknown a three-point circuit is required. Remember the structure of Sappho's fragment 31: an "erotic triangle" where the three components of desire all become visible at once in a sort of electrification. We suggested, during our consideration of this poem, that its triangular shape is more than an arbitrary elegance on the part of the poet. Desire cannot be perceived apart from these three angles. Aristotle's conception of *phantasia* may help us to see how this is so. On his view, every desiring mind reaches out toward its object by means of an imaginative action. If this is true, no lover, poet or otherwise, can hold his desire aloof from the fictive, triangulating enterprise revealed to us by Sappho in fragment 31. "Eros makes every man a poet" says the ancient wisdom (Eur. *Sthen.*, *TGF*, fr.663; Pl. *Symp.* 196e).

Eros is always a story in which lover, beloved and the difference between them interact. The interaction is a fiction arranged by the mind of the lover. It carries an emotional charge both hateful and delicious and emits a light like knowledge. No one took a more clear-eyed view of this matter than Sappho. No one caught its features more accurately in adjectives. We have seen, in the foregoing pages, some of the force of her neologism *glukupikron*, 'bittersweet.' Here is another label she devised to characterize erotic experience:

τὸν Ἔρωτα Σωκράτης σοφιστὴν λέγει, Σαπφὼ μυθοπλόκον.

Sokrates calls Eros a Sophist, but Sappho calls him "weaver of fictions" [*mythoplokon*].

says Maximus of Tyre (18.9; Sappho, *LP*, fr. 188). The adjective *mythoplokos*, as well as the context in which Maximus has preserved it for us, draws together some significant aspects of Eros. For Sappho, the desirability of desire seems to be bound up with the fictional process that she calls the "weaving of myth." Sokrates, on the other hand, sees in this process something resembling sophistry. How intriguing this alignment of Sappho and Sokrates, this bracketing of the storyteller with the professor of wisdom: they have Eros in common. How so?

In our readings of Greek texts, we have followed the traces of an ancient analogy between the wooing of knowledge and the wooing of love, from its earliest relic in the Homeric verb *mnaomai*. Let us reconsider this analogy, designating Sappho and Sokrates to represent its two poles. As soon as we do so we meet a difficulty. Sokrates, by his own testimony, prefers to collapse the two poles into one. It is a single question that arches through his life, a single research in which comprehension of the truly real and pursuit of the truly desirable are identified. Twice in the Platonic dialogues he speaks about his search for wisdom and asserts that his knowledge, such as it is, is *nothing but* a knowledge of "erotic things" (*ta erōtika*: *Symp.* 177d; *Theag.* 128b). He does not tell us in either passage what he means by *ta erōtika*, "erotic things." But we can deduce it from the story of his life.

He loved to ask questions. He loved to hear answers, construct arguments, test definitions, uncover riddles and watch them unfold out of one another in a structure opening down through the *logos* like a spiralling road (*Phdr.* 274a; cf. 272c) or a vertigo (*Soph.* 264c). He loved, that is, the process of coming to know. Concerning this love he is frank and precise. He tells us exactly where Eros is located in the process of knowing or thinking. Eros lies at the intersection of two principles of reasoning, for *logos* proceeds in two simultaneous operations. On the one hand, the reasoning mind must perceive and bring together certain scattered particulars, in order to make clear by definition the thing it wishes to explain. This is the activity of "collection" (*synagōgē*: *Phdr.* 265d-e). On the other hand, it is necessary to divide things up by classes, where the natural joints are: this activity is "division" (*diaeresis*, 265e).

That is to say, we think by projecting sameness upon difference, by drawing things together in a relation or idea while at the same time maintaining the distinctions between them. A thinking mind is not swallowed up by what it comes to know. It reaches out to grasp something related to itself and to its present knowledge (and so knowable in some degree) but also separate from itself and from its present knowledge (not identical with these). In any act of thinking, the mind must reach across this space between known and unknown, linking one to the other but also keeping visible their difference. It is an erotic space. To reach across it is tricky; a kind of stereoscopy seems to be required. We have studied this stereoscopic activity in other contexts, for example, in Sappho's fragment 31. The same subterfuge which we have called an "erotic ruse" in novels and poems now appears to constitute the very structure of human thinking. When the mind reaches out to know, the space of desire opens and a necessary fiction transpires.

It is in this space, at the point where the two principles

of reasoning intersect, that Sokrates locates Eros. He describes "collection and division" as the activity that empowers him to speak and to think (*Phdr.* 266b). And he alleges that he is *in love with* this activity:

Τούτων δὴ ἔγωγε αὐτός τε ἐραστής, ὦ Φαῖδρε, τῶν διαιρέσεων καὶ συναγωγῶν. . . .

The fact is, Phaedrus, I am myself a lover [*erastēs*] of these divisions and collections. (*Phdr.* 266b; cf. *Phlb.* 16b)

That is a startling thing to say. But he must have been serious: he spent his life on the activity, impelled by a single question. It was a question stirred up in him by the Pythia at Delphi when she, according to the well-known story recounted in Plato's *Apology*, pronounced Sokrates to be the wisest of men. The pronouncement troubled Sokrates. After some considerable research and reflection, however, he came to a conclusion about what the oracle meant:

ἔοικα γοῦν τούτου γε σμικρῷ τινι αὐτῷ τούτῳ σοφώτερος εἶναι, ὅτι ἃ μὴ οἶδα οὐδὲ οἴομαι εἰδέναι.

In this one small thing at least it seems I am wiser—that I do not think I know what I do not know. (*Ap.* 21d)

A power to see the difference between what is known and what is unknown constitutes Sokrates' wisdom and motivated his searching life. The activity of reaching out for that difference is one with which he admits he is in love.

From the testimony of lovers like Sokrates or Sappho we can construct what it would be like to live in a city of no desire. Both the philosopher and the poet find themselves describing Eros in images of wings and metaphors of flying, for desire is a movement that carries yearning hearts from over here to over there, launching the mind on a story. In the city without desire such flights are unimaginable. Wings are kept clipped. The known and the unknown learn to align themselves one behind the other so that, provided you are positioned at the proper angle, they seem to be one and the same. If there *were* a visible difference, you might find it hard to say so, for the useful verb *mnaomai* will have come to mean 'a fact is a fact.' To reach for something else than the facts will carry you beyond this city and perhaps, as for Sokrates, beyond this world. It is a high-risk proposition, as Sokrates saw quite clearly, to reach for the difference between known and unknown. He thought the risk worthwhile, because he was in love with the wooing itself. And who is not?

Bibliography

Auden, W. H. *Collected Poems*. Edited by E. Mendelson. New York, 1976.

Augustine. *Sancti Aureli Augustini Confessionum Libri Tredecim*. Edited by P. Knoll. Leipzig, 1896.

Barthes, R. *A Lover's Discourse: Fragments*. Translated by R. Howard. New York, 1978.

Basho Matsuo. *The Narrow Road to the Deep North and Other Travel Sketches*. Translated by Nobayuki Yuasa. New York, 1966.

Baxandall, M. *Painting and Experience in Fifteenth Century Italy: A Primer in the Social History of Pictorial Style*. Oxford, 1972.

Blass, F., ed. *Isocrates Orationes*. Leipzig, 1898.

Burnet, J. *Platonis Opera*. 6 vols. Oxford, 1902–1906.

Burnett, A. P. *Three Archaic Poets: Archilochus, Alcaeus, Sappho*. London, 1983.

Busse, A. *Elias in Aristotelis Categorias commentaria*. Berlin, 1900.

Calvino, I. *The Nonexistent Knight*. Translated by A. Colquhoun. New York and London, 1962.

Carrière, J. *Théognis: Poèmes élégiaques*. Paris, 1962.

Cartledge, P. "Literacy in the Spartan Oligarchy." *Journal of Hellenic Studies* 98 (1978), 25-37.

Cohen, J. *Structure du langage poétique*. Paris, 1966.

Coldstream, J. N. *Geometric Greece*. London, 1977.

Cole, S. G. "Could Greek Women Read and Write?" *Women's Studies* 8 (1981), 129-55.

Colonna, A., ed. *Heliodori Aethiopica*. Rome, 1938.

Coulon, V. *Aristophane*. 5 vols. Paris, 1967–1972.

Dalmeyda, G. *Longus: Pastorales.* Paris, 1934.

Davison, J. A. "Literature and Literacy in Ancient Greece." *Phoenix* 16 (1962), 141-233. Reprinted in *From Archilochus to Pindar*, 86-128. London, 1968.

De Beauvoir, S. *The Second Sex.* Translated by H. M. Parshley. New York, 1953.

Denniston, J. D. *The Greek Particles.* 2nd ed. Oxford, 1954.

De Vries, G. J. *A Commentary on the Phaedrus of Plato.* Amsterdam, 1969.

Dickinson, E. *The Complete Poems.* Edited by T. H. Johnson. Boston, 1960.

Diels, H. *Die Fragmente der Vorsokratiker, griechisch und deutsch.* 3 vols. Berlin, 1959–1960.

Dodds, E. R. "A Fragment of a Greek Novel." In *Studies in Honour of Gilbert Norwood*, ed. M. E. White, 133-53. Toronto, 1952.

Donne, J. *The Complete English Poems.* Edited by A. J. Smith. Harmondsworth, 1971.

Dover, K. J. *Greek Homosexuality.* Cambridge, Mass., 1978.

Dübner, F., ed. *Himerius Orationes.* Paris, 1849.

Edmonds, J. M., ed. *Elegy and Iambus . . . with the Anacreontea.* 2 vols. Cambridge, Mass., 1961.

Erdman, D. V., ed. *The Notebooks of William Blake.* New York, 1977.

Finnegan, R. *Oral Poetry: Its Nature, Significance, and Social Context.* Cambridge, 1977.

Flaubert, G. *Madame Bovary: Moeurs de province.* 2 vols. Paris, 1857.

Fondation Hardt. *Entretiens sur l'antiquité classique*, vol. 10: *Archiloque.* Geneva, 1963.

Foucault, M. *The Order of Things: An Archaeology of the Human Sciences.* New York, 1973.

Fränkel, H. *Early Greek Poetry and Philosophy.* Translated by M. Hadas and J. Willis. New York and London, 1973.

Gaisford, T., ed. *Ioannis Stobaei Florilegium.* 4 vols. Oxford, 1822.

Gaselee, S., ed. *Achilles Tatius: Clitophon and Leucippe.* New York, 1917.

Gelb, I. J. *Study of Writing.* rev. ed. Chicago, 1963.

Girard, R. *Deceit, Desire, and the Novel: Self and Other in Literary Structure.* Translated by Y. Freccero. Baltimore and London, 1965.

Gomme, A. W. "Interpretations of Some Poems of Alkaios and Sappho." *Journal of Hellenic Studies* 77 (1957), 259-60.

Goody, J., ed. *The Domestication of the Savage Mind.* Cambridge, 1977.

———. *Literacy in Traditional Societies.* Cambridge, 1968.

Gow, A. S. *Theocritus.* 2 vols. Cambridge, 1952.

Graff, H. J. *Literacy in History: An Interdisciplinary Research Bibliography.* New York, 1981.

Harvey, D. "Greeks and Romans Learn to Write." In *Communication Arts in the Ancient World,* ed. E. A. Havelock and J. P. Hershbell, 63-80. New York, 1978.

Havelock, E. A. *The Greek Concept of Justice.* Cambridge, Mass., 1978.

———. *The Literate Revolution in Greece and Its Cultural Consequences.* Princeton, 1982.

———. "The Oral Composition of Greek Drama." *Quaderni Urbinati di Cultura Classica* 35 (1980), 61-112.

———. *Origins of Western Literacy.* Toronto, 1976.

———. *Preface to Plato.* Cambridge, Mass., 1963.

———. *Prologue to Greek Literacy.* Cincinnati, 1971.

Havelock, E. A., and J. P. Hershbell. *Communication Arts in the Ancient World.* New York, 1978.

Heiserman, A. *The Novel before the Novel.* Chicago, 1977.

Heubeck, A. von. "Die homerische Göttersprache."

Würzburger Jahrbücher für die Altertumswissenschaft 4 (1949-50), 197-218.

Hilgard, A. *Grammatici Graeci.* 3 vols. Leipzig, 1901.

Hodge, A. T. "The Mystery of Apollo's E at Delphi." *American Journal of Archaeology* 85 (1981), 83-84.

Holloway, J. "Cone." *The Times Literary Supplement,* 24 October 1975, 1262.

Humboldt, W. von. *Gesammelte Werke.* 6 vols. Berlin, 1848.

Innis, H. A. *The Bias of Communication.* Toronto, 1951.

Jacoby, F. *Die Fragmente der griechischen Historiker.* 15 vols. Berlin, 1923–1930; Leiden, 1943–1958.

Jaeger, W., ed. *Aristoteles Metaphysica.* Oxford, 1957.

———. *Paideia.* 3 vols. Berlin and Leipzig, 1934–1947.

Jebb, R. C. *Sophocles.* 7 vols. 1883–1896. Reprint. Amsterdam, 1962.

Jeffrey, L. H. *The Local Scripts of Archaic Greece.* Oxford, 1961.

Jenkins, I. "Is There Life after Marriage? A Study of the Abduction Motif in Vase Paintings of the Athenian Wedding Ceremony." *Bulletin of the Institute for Classical Studies* 30 (1983), 137-45.

Jenkyns, R. *Three Classical Poets: Sappho, Catullus, and Juvenal.* Cambridge, Mass., 1982.

Jensen, H. *Die Schrift in Vergangenheit und Gegenwart.* Berlin, 1969.

Johnston, A. "The Extent and Use of Literacy: The Archaeological Evidence." In *The Greek Renaissance of the Eighth Century B.C.: Tradition and Innovation,* ed. R. Hägg, 63-68. Stockholm, 1983.

Kafka, F. *The Complete Stories.* Edited by N. N. Glatzer. New York, 1971.

Kaibel, G., ed. *Athenaei Naucratitae Dipnosophistarum.* 3 vols. Leipzig, 1887–1890.

Kawabata, Y. *Beauty and Sadness.* Translated by H. Hibbet. New York, 1975.

Keats, J. *Poems.* London, 1817.

Kenyon, F. G. *The Palaeography of Greek Papyri.* Oxford, 1899.

Kierkegaard, S. *Either/Or: A Fragment of Life.* Translated by D. F. Swenson and L. M. Swenson. Princeton and London, 1944.

Knox, B.M.W. "Silent Reading in Antiquity." *Greek, Roman, and Byzantine Studies* 9 (1968), 421-35.

Kock, T., ed. *Comicorum Atticorum Fragmenta.* 3 vols. Leipzig, 1880–1888.

Kundera, M. *The Book of Laughter and Forgetting.* Translated by M. H. Heim. New York, 1980.

Labarrière, J.-L. "Imagination humaine et imagination animale chez Aristote." *Phoenix* 29 (1984), 17-49.

Lacan, J. *Ecrits.* Paris, 1966.

Lang, M. *The Athenian Agora XXI.* Princeton, 1976.

Lobel, E., and D. Page, eds. *Poetarum Lesbiorum Fragmenta.* Oxford, 1955.

Lucas, D. W., ed. *Aristotle: Poetics.* Oxford, 1968.

Massa, E. *Andreas Capellanus: Il libro amore nel Medioevo.* 2 vols. Rome, 1976.

Monro, D. B., and T. W. Allen. *Homeri Opera.* 5 vols. Oxford, 1920.

Montaigne, M. de. *The Essays.* Translated by J. Florio. London, 1603.

Murray, G. *Aeschyli Septem Quae Supersunt Tragoediae.* Oxford, 1937.

———. *Euripidis Fabulae.* 3 vols. Oxford, 1913–1915.

Musso, O. *Michele Psello: Nozioni paradossali.* Naples, 1977.

Mylonas, G. E. "Prehistoric Greek Scripts." *Archaeology* 4 (1948), 210-19.

Nauck, A. *Tragicorum Graecorum Fragmenta.* 2nd ed. Leipzig, 1889.

Nietzsche, F. *The Will to Power.* Translated by W. Kaufmann and R. J. Hollingdale. New York, 1967.

Nussbaum, M. "Fictions of the Soul." *Philosophy and Literature* 7 (1983), 145-61.

Onians, R. B. *The Origins of European Thought about the Body, the Mind, the Soul, the World, Time, and Fate.* Cambridge, 1951.

Page, D. L., ed. *Poetae Melici Graeci.* Oxford, 1962.

———. *Select Papyri.* London and Cambridge, Mass., 1932.

Parke, H. W. *The Delphic Oracle.* 2 vols. Oxford, 1956.

———. *The Oracles of Zeus.* Oxford, 1967.

Paton, W. R. *The Greek Anthology.* 5 vols. London and New York, 1916–1926.

Perry, B. E. *The Ancient Romances.* Berkeley and Los Angeles, 1967.

Petrarch, F. *I Trionfi.* Venice, 1874.

Pfeiffer, R., ed. *Callimachus.* 2 vols. Oxford, 1965.

Pomeroy, S. B. "Technikai kai Mousikai." *American Journal of Ancient History* 2 (1977), 15-28.

Pushkin, A. *Eugene Onegin.* Translated by V. Nabokov. 4 vols. Princeton, 1964.

Quinn, K., ed. *Catullus: The Poems.* London, 1970.

Race, W. H. " 'That Man' in Sappho fr. 31 LP." *Classical Antiquity* 2 (1983), 92-102.

Radt, S., ed. *Tragicorum Graecorum Fragmenta IV: Sophocles.* Gottingen, 1977.

Ricoeur, P. "The Metaphorical Process as Cognition, Imagination, and Feeling." *Critical Inquiry* 5 (1978), 143-58.

Rilke, R. M. *Selected Poetry.* Edited by S. Mitchell. New York, 1984.

Robb, K. "Poetic Sources of the Greek Alphabet." In *Communication Arts in the Ancient World,* ed. E. A. Havelock and J. P. Hershbell, 23-36. New York, 1978.

Robbins, E. " 'Everytime I Look at You . . .' Sappho Thirty-One." *Transactions of the American Philological Association* 110 (1980), 255-61.

Rocha-Pereira, M. H. *Pausaniae Graeciae Descriptio.* 3 vols. Leipzig, 1973.

Ross, W. D. *Aristotelis Ars Rhetorica*. Oxford, 1959.

———. *Aristotelis De Anima*. Oxford, 1956.

———. *Aristotelis Parva Naturalia*. Oxford, 1955.

———. *Aristotelis Physica*. Oxford, 1950.

———. *Aristotelis Politica*. Oxford, 1957.

———. *Aristotle's Metaphysics*. 2 vols. Oxford, 1924.

Russell, D. A. *Libellus de sublimitate Dionysio Longino fere adscriptus*. Oxford, 1968.

Sartre, J.-P. *Being and Nothingness*. Translated by H. E. Barnes. New York, 1956.

———. *Sketch for a Theory of the Emotions*. Translated by P. Mairet. London, 1962.

Saussure, F. de. *Cours de linguistique générale*. Paris, 1971.

Searle, J. R. "Las Meninas and the Paradoxes of Pictorial Representation." *Critical Inquiry* 6 (1980), 477-88.

Seaton, R. C., ed. *Apollonii Rhodii Argonautica*. Oxford, 1900.

Sirvinou-Inwood, C. "The Young Abductor of the Lokrian Pinakes." *Bulletin of the Institute for Classical Studies* 20 (1973), 12-21.

Slater, M. *Dickens and Women*. London, 1983.

Snell, B. *The Discovery of the Mind in Greek Philosophy and Literature*. Translated by T. G. Rosenmeyer. New Haven, 1953.

Snell, B., and H. Maehler, eds. *Pindari Carmina cum Fragmentis*. 2 vols. Leipzig, 1975–1980.

Snodgrass, A. M. *Archaic Greece: The Age of Experiment*. London, 1980.

Solmsen, F. *Hesiodi Theogonia, Opera et Dies, Scutum*. Oxford, 1970.

Staiger, E. *Grundbegriffe der Poetik*. Zurich, 1946.

Stanford, W. B. *Greek Metaphor: Studies in Theory and Practice*. Oxford, 1936.

Stendahl (M. H. Beyle). *The Life of Henri Brulard*. Translated by J. Stewart and B. Knight. Middlesex, 1973.

Stendahl (M. H. Beyle). *Love.* Translated by G. Sale and S. Sale. New York, 1957.

Stolz, B. A., and R. S. Shannon III, eds. *Oral Literature and the Formula.* Ann Arbor, 1976.

Svenbro, J. *La Parole et le marbre: Aux origines de la poétique grecque.* Lund, 1976.

Tanizaki, J. *The Secret History of the Lord of Musashi and Arrowroot.* Translated by A. H. Chambers. New York, 1982.

Tolstoy, L. N. *Anna Karenina.* Translated by R. Edmonds. New York, 1978.

Turner, E. G. *Athenian Books in the Fifth and Fourth Centuries B.C.* London, 1952.

Waiblinger, F. P. *Historia Apollonii regis Tyri.* Munich, 1978.

Weil, S. *The Simone Weil Reader.* Edited by G. A. Panichas. New York, 1977.

Welty, E. *One Writer's Beginnings.* Cambridge, Mass., 1984.

West, M. L. "Burning Sappho." *Maia* 22 (1970), 307-30.

———. *Hesiod: Theogony.* Oxford, 1966.

———. *Iambi et Elegi Graeci.* 2 vols. Oxford, 1971–1972.

Woodhead, A. G. *The Study of Greek Inscriptions.* 2nd ed. Cambridge, 1981.

Woolf, V. *The Waves.* New York, 1931.

Index of Passages Discussed

General Index

absence and presence, 11, 16, 18, 52, 62, 72, 86, 91-92, 96, 99, 104, 111, 117, 169, 171
aidōs, 20-21, 25, 79-80
Alkibiades, 5, 22-23, 66, 75
alphabet, 41-44, 46, 51, 53-55, 57-59, 94, 98, 105, 108. *See also* reading and writing
Andromeda, 93-94
Anna Karenina, 4, 64, 66
Aphrodite, 4-6, 32, 77, 80-81, 148
apples, 20, 26-29, 69, 87-90, 109, 111, 166
Archilochos, 8, 42, 46-52, 99
Atalanta, 19

Beauvoir, Simone de, 11
Bellerophon, 101-106
blind point, 71-72, 75, 82, 90-91, 95, 104-105, 110-11, 116, 122, 145, 158, 166
boundaries, 30, 40-41, 50-51, 71
boustrophēdon, 58-59
Bovary, Emma, 65

Calvino, Italo, 65
chastity, 22, 80
cicadas, 138-39, 150, 159
collection and division, 171-72
consonants, 47, 53-55, 57, 61, 162. *See also* vowels
contradiction, 3, 9, 10-11, 23-24, 84, 89, 92
coup de foudre, 19
crystallization, 64-65

Dante, 90, 106-107
décolletage, 28
deltos, 100
dēute, 118-20, 149
Dickens, Charles, 106-107

General Index

reach, 25-29, 32, 52, 63, 68, 69, 71, 85-86, 88, 94, 95, 109, 166, 168-69, 171, 173. *See also* pursuit and flight
reading and writing, 4, 42-44, 46, 50-51, 53, 55-61, 77-78, 81, 85-87, 89, 91, 93-109, 120-21, 130-35, 141-43, 145-47, 151-54, 164-66, 168. *See also* literacy
ruse, 16-18, 33, 63, 82, 84, 91, 95, 171

Sappho, 3-5, 8-9, 11-12, 14-16, 18, 21, 26-27, 32, 38-39, 62, 66, 69, 83, 98, 107, 119-20, 127, 156, 166, 169-72
Sartre, Jean-Paul, 10, 40
Saussure, Ferdinand de, 51
self, 30-33, 35-41, 43-45, 50-51, 62, 66-67, 69, 71, 74, 109, 135-36, 147-49, 154-56, 165
shift of distance, 17, 23, 73, 75, 81, 85, 86, 90, 94-95, 97
skutalē, 99
Snell, Bruno, 37-38, 41
Sokrates, 22, 23, 33, 34, 35, 37, 65, 70, 122, 126, 127, 128, 131, 132, 134, 136, 137, 138, 141, 142, 143, 144, 149, 151, 152, 153, 154, 159, 160, 161, 162, 163, 165, 166, 170, 171, 172, 173
sōphrosynē, 150, 154, 159
Stendahl, 63-65
stereoscopy, 17, 73, 85, 90, 118, 126, 166, 171
symbolization, 52-54, 61, 75, 87-88, 94, 108, 146
symbolon, 75

time, 4, 29, 88, 111, 113-22, 124-28, 130, 133-37, 139-46, 149-53, 157, 159, 162, 165
triangle, 13, 16-18, 23, 33, 37, 62, 69, 72, 77, 79-80, 85-87, 91-97, 102-103, 105, 109, 143, 169
Tristan and Iseult, 23

Velázquez, Diego, 71, 74, 82
vertigo, xi, 72, 85, 116-17
vowels, 17, 53-54, 56, 58, 162. *See also* consonants

weddings, 24-27, 29, 80, 91
Weil, Simone, 10
Welty, Eudora, 55, 106-107
wholeness, 31-33, 36, 38, 41, 68
wings, 13, 49, 89, 108, 120, 148, 152, 155-57, 159, 161, 163, 172
wooing, 71, 75, 87-88, 97, 103, 108, 170, 173
Woolf, Virginia, 36-39, 66

Zeno, 81, 89, 166, 168
Zeus, 31, 100

SELECTED DALKEY ARCHIVE PAPERBACKS

PETROS ABATZOGLOU, *What Does Mrs. Freeman Want?*
PIERRE ALBERT-BIROT, *Grabinoulor.*
YUZ ALESHKOVSKY, *Kangaroo.*
SVETLANA ALEXIEVICH, *Voices from Chernobyl.*
FELIPE ALFAU, *Chromos.*
  Locos.
IVAN ÂNGELO, *The Celebration.*
  The Tower of Glass.
DAVID ANTIN, *Talking.*
DJUNA BARNES, *Ladies Almanack.*
  Ryder.
JOHN BARTH, *LETTERS.*
  Sabbatical.
DONALD BARTHELME, *Paradise.*
SVETISLAV BASARA, *Chinese Letter.*
ANDREI BITOV, *Pushkin House.*
LOUIS PAUL BOON, *Chapel Road.*
ROGER BOYLAN, *Killoyle.*
IGNÁCIO DE LOYOLA BRANDÃO, *Zero.*
CHRISTINE BROOKE-ROSE, *Amalgamemnon.*
BRIGID BROPHY, *In Transit.*
MEREDITH BROSNAN, *Mr. Dynamite.*
GERALD L. BRUNS,
  Modern Poetry and the Idea of Language.
GABRIELLE BURTON, *Heartbreak Hotel.*
MICHEL BUTOR, *Degrees.*
  Mobile.
  Portrait of the Artist as a Young Ape.
G. CABRERA INFANTE, *Infante's Inferno.*
  Three Trapped Tigers.
JULIETA CAMPOS, *The Fear of Losing Eurydice.*
ANNE CARSON, *Eros the Bittersweet.*
CAMILO JOSÉ CELA, *The Family of Pascual Duarte.*
  The Hive.
LOUIS-FERDINAND CÉLINE, *Castle to Castle.*
  London Bridge.
  North.
  Rigadoon.
HUGO CHARTERIS, *The Tide Is Right.*
JEROME CHARYN, *The Tar Baby.*
MARC CHOLODENKO, *Mordechai Schamz.*
EMILY HOLMES COLEMAN, *The Shutter of Snow.*
ROBERT COOVER, *A Night at the Movies.*
STANLEY CRAWFORD, *Some Instructions to My Wife.*
ROBERT CREELEY, *Collected Prose.*
RENÉ CREVEL, *Putting My Foot in It.*
RALPH CUSACK, *Cadenza.*
SUSAN DAITCH, *L.C.*
  Storytown.
NIGEL DENNIS, *Cards of Identity.*
PETER DIMOCK,
  A Short Rhetoric for Leaving the Family.
ARIEL DORFMAN, *Konfidenz*
COLEMAN DOWELL, *The Houses of Children.*
  Island People.
  Too Much Flesh and Jabez.
RIKKI DUCORNET, *The Complete Butcher's Tales.*
  The Fountains of Neptune.
  The Jade Cabinet.
  Phosphor in Dreamland.
  The Stain.
  The Word "Desire."
WILLIAM EASTLAKE, *The Bamboo Bed.*
  Castle Keep.
  Lyric of the Circle Heart.
JEAN ECHENOZ, *Chopin's Move.*
STANLEY ELKIN, *A Bad Man.*
  Boswell: A Modern Comedy.
  Criers and Kibitzers, Kibitzers and Criers.
  The Dick Gibson Show.
  The Franchiser.
  George Mills.
  The Living End.
  The MacGuffin.
  The Magic Kingdom.

Mrs. Ted Bliss.
The Rabbi of Lud.
Van Gogh's Room at Arles.
. ANNIE ERNAUX, *Cleaned Out.*
LAUREN FAIRBANKS, *Muzzle Thyself.*
  Sister Carrie.
LESLIE A. FIEDLER,
  Love and Death in the American Novel.
GUSTAVE FLAUBERT, *Bouvard and Pécuchet.*
FORD MADOX FORD, *The March of Literature.*
CARLOS FUENTES, *Christopher Unborn.*
  Terra Nostra.
  Where the Air Is Clear.
JANICE GALLOWAY, *Foreign Parts.*
  The Trick Is to Keep Breathing.
WILLIAM H. GASS, *The Tunnel.*
  Willie Masters' Lonesome Wife.
ETIENNE GILSON, *The Arts of the Beautiful.*
  Forms and Substances in the Arts.
C. S. GISCOMBE, *Giscome Road.*
  Here.
DOUGLAS GLOVER, *Bad News of the Heart.*
  The Enamoured Knight.
KAREN ELIZABETH GORDON, *The Red Shoes.*
GEORGI GOSPODINOV, *Natural Novel.*
PATRICK GRAINVILLE, *The Cave of Heaven.*
HENRY GREEN, *Blindness.*
  Concluding.
  Doting.
  Nothing.
JIŘÍ GRUŠA, *The Questionnaire.*
JOHN HAWKES, *Whistlejacket.*
AIDAN HIGGINS, *A Bestiary.*
  Flotsam and Jetsam.
  Langrishe, Go Down.
  Scenes from a Receding Past.
  Windy Arbours.
ALDOUS HUXLEY, *Antic Hay.*
  Crome Yellow.
  Point Counter Point.
  Those Barren Leaves.
  Time Must Have a Stop.
MIKHAIL IOSSEL AND JEFF PARKER, EDS., *Amerika:*
  Contemporary Russians View
  the United States.
GERT JONKE, *Geometric Regional Novel.*
JACQUES JOUET, *Mountain R.*
HUGH KENNER, *The Counterfeiters.*
  Flaubert, Joyce and Beckett:
  The Stoic Comedians.
DANILO KIŠ, *Garden, Ashes.*
  A Tomb for Boris Davidovich.
NOBUO KOJIMA, *Embracing Family.*
TADEUSZ KONWICKI, *A Minor Apocalypse.*
  The Polish Complex.
MENIS KOUMANDAREAS, *Koula.*
ELAINE KRAF, *The Princess of 72nd Street.*
JIM KRUSOE, *Iceland.*
EWA KURYLUK, *Century 21.*
VIOLETTE LEDUC, *La Bâtarde.*
DEBORAH LEVY, *Billy and Girl.*
  Pillow Talk in Europe and Other Places.
JOSÉ LEZAMA LIMA, *Paradiso.*
OSMAN LINS, *Avalovara.*
  The Queen of the Prisons of Greece.
ALF MAC LOCHLAINN, *The Corpus in the Library.*
  Out of Focus.
RON LOEWINSOHN, *Magnetic Field(s).*
D. KEITH MANO, *Take Five.*
BEN MARCUS, *The Age of Wire and String.*
WALLACE MARKFIELD, *Teitlebaum's Window.*
  To an Early Grave.
DAVID MARKSON, *Reader's Block.*
  Springer's Progress.
  Wittgenstein's Mistress.

FOR A FULL LIST OF PUBLICATIONS, VISIT:
www.dalkeyarchive.com

SELECTED DALKEY ARCHIVE PAPERBACKS

FOR A FULL LIST OF PUBLICATIONS, VISIT:

www.dalkeyarchive.com